Mary
A Focus for Unity
for all Christians?

Sermons
and Conference Talks
presented both at Lourdes
and at Nettuno
in 2008

The Confraternity of the Blessed Sacrament
www.confraternity.org.uk

and

The Catholic League
www.thecatholicleague.org

*have made financial contributions
towards the production costs of this publication*

© The Society of Mary, 2009

Some images in the Lourdes picture supplement are © Lacaze

British Library Cataloguing in Publication Data

ISBN 978-0-9562537-0-5

Printed in England by POSTPRINT
Taverner House, Harling Road, East Harling, Norfolk NR16 2QR

CONTENTS

Foreword

WHETHER we recognise it or not, all of us who bear the name of Christ share a relationship with Mary – our eldest sister in faith, our mother in love and a sign of hope fulfilled. Celebrating Our Lady should not be a marginal eccentricity for us, but a normal and joyful element in our affirmation of common belief and thanksgiving.

The Society of Mary has done so much to keep this message alive in a church that often seems a bit embarrassed by the idea of rejoicing in Mary's triumphant faith and loving participation with us in the Body of her Son; and it is part of this witness that the Society has also built friendships with Christian communities outside Britain and outside our own Communion, so as to deepen our awareness of how Our Lady finds ways of bringing believers together – both in celebration of the Good News and at the foot of the Cross.

This book tells us something of the history and the charism of the Society, but it also contains the record of two particular pilgrimages in 2008 which expressed with special intensity the hopes and prayers of the members. The pilgrimage to Nettuno reflects the wish to heal some of the memories of the past – memories of an age when the reaction against abuses of Marian devotion led to a terrible rejection of some of the most evangelical and nourishing elements in Christian practice. But in addition to this event of reconciliation and reparation, 2008 also saw the pilgrimage to Lourdes to take part in the 150th anniversary of the devotion there. For all who took part, this was an unforgettable experience of shared inspiration, made all the more memorable by the unstinted warmth and generosity of our hosts locally.

Even in a Church that is painfully divided – and in which divisions seem to grow no less as time goes on – there are moments when Mary's faith, hope and love still draw us powerfully together to recall us to the fundamental of our belief in the Word made flesh for our salvation. The journeys out of which these pages come were very much that kind of experience for those who shared them. I hope and pray that they will inspire and encourage others in their witness to the one who first welcomed the incarnate Lord and served him with joy.

✠ *Rowan Cantuar:*
Easter, 2009

The Wonder of Our Lady of Grace

The Italian connection

THE SHRINES to Our Lady in Ipswich and Nettuno may seem worlds apart but they are in fact bound together by a seafaring tale of storm and shipwreck; and today, they are honoured by pilgrims from the two towns.

It was one of the greatest single acts of desecration that England has ever seen, and it happened in Chelsea, then a rural enclave west of teeming Tudor London, just short of 500 years ago.

Piled high in the grounds of the house of perhaps the most powerful man in the country, bar King Henry VIII himself, were 84 hitherto much venerated statues of Our Lady. They had been gathered from shrines from all corners of the kingdom by men working for Thomas Cromwell, during his two year countrywide "visitations" to abbeys and monasteries to preside over their dissolution, and brought to his house. There on 20th September 1538, Cromwell, Henry's chief minister, gave the sign and the burning began, consigning to the flames of the Reformation such treasures as the Marian statues of Willesden and of England's premier shrine to the Virgin, Walsingham.

Second only to Walsingham at that time was the Shrine of Our Lady of Grace in Ipswich, and it was assumed that her statue was also consumed by Cromwell's bonfire. But according to local archives she was in fact spirited away across the sea to the Italian port of Nettuno, some 40 miles south of Rome, whence she continued to be venerated throughout the centuries and to where for the past 30 years local faithful have been joined by modern pilgrims from Ipswich.

More recently, there have been reciprocal visits between Nettuno and the restored shine in Ipswich. In early May 2008 some 70 pilgrims of several denominations in Ipswich, led by the Anglican Bishops of Whitby and Richborough, and accompanied by the Mayor of Ipswich, visited the shrine at Nettuno, and that month 38 Nettunese made a return pilgrimage to Ipswich.

The history of the shrine of Our Lady of Grace dates from the beginning of the twelfth century, when Ipswich had, among its 39 churches, a small chapel, which came to be known as the Shrine of Our Lady of Grace. Our Lady was evidently much revered in Ipswich as no fewer than five parish churches are dedicated to Mary.

Pilgrims came to Ipswich (and miracles sometimes happened). Many famous people visited, including Catherine of Aragon, Henry VIII himself, Sir Thomas More and, of course, the Ipswich-born Cardinal Wolsey. Containing a beautifully carved figure of the Blessed Virgin Mary and Child, the shrine regrettably all but disappeared following Cromwell's visitations. All that is left is a plaque on the wall of a shop in a small byway called Lady Lane.

Thomas Wolsey was, the son of an Ipswich butcher and, even when he had attained national importance, he retained a great affection for his home town. He founded a college that was set to rival the colleges of Oxford and Cambridge; by 1529 the building was almost complete, and the staff appointed.

To ensure that his college was closely linked with the Shrine of Our Lady of Grace, he planned a great procession between the two for 8th September 1529. The rehearsal took place the night before, but due to torrential rain the actual procession never materialised. Wolsey then fell from grace, and his college was demolished almost as soon as it was completed, with a small gateway being the only part remaining today.

During the Reformation, along with the spoils from all the other Marian shrines, many of the statues were destroyed, but some priceless relics and holy objects from shrines did escape the destruction and were sold off to refill the king's depleted coffers. Others, however, were hidden away to await more peaceful times and it may be via this route that the Ipswich figure of Our Lady of Grace escaped the inferno. For in Nettuno, the Sanctuary of Our Lady of Grace contains the very same figure, authenticated by several historians, as the "English Lady" of Ipswich. On the base of the figure are carved the words "Thou art gracious" in old English.

The story goes that somehow sailors had managed to smuggle the statue on-board ship to evade the king's men. Accounts in the local archives suggest that the ship, of Spanish design, was caught in a storm off the coast of Italy and, fearing certain shipwreck, the crew offered prayers to Our Lady and the captain headed for the small port of Nettuno. When the bad weather subsided the captain made moves to leave, but the wind rose again to gale force, and the ship returned to port. On the third attempt to leave it was then understood that Our Lady wished to remain in Nettuno.

The figure was given to the inhabitants of Nettuno and rested in a small chapel by the port, outside the fortified town. The original sanctuary was replaced on several occasions, the last being after the Allied landings in the Second World War when the town was very badly damaged. Our Lady of Grace was spared as she was removed to Rome for safekeeping. Today there is a large sanctuary, where Our Lady has pride of place above the main altar, while S. Maria Goretti lies in the crypt cared for by Passionist fathers.

After all these centuries the figure is still carried each year by members of the Confraternity of Our Lady of Grace in procession from the sanctuary to the Church of S. Giovanni in the town centre where she remains for a week.

The statue is decorated with lights and surrounded by figures of angels, so it takes eight men with frequent changes, to carry the litter. At certain points on the route Our Lady pauses to acknowledge the crowds and vast firework displays erupt. The procession made up of children, visiting groups, clergy and local dignitaries is usually about a mile in length, and so the front reaches the destination even before Our Lady leaves the sanctuary.

In 1975 the first pilgrimage from Ipswich to Nettuno took place, and the ecumenical Guild of Our Lady of Ipswich was formed to be a focus of church unity. In 2001 the Shrine of Our Lady of Grace in Ipswich was restored in the Church of S. Mary at the Elms, a beautiful Anglo-Catholic church, very near the original shrine. A new replica statue was carved by Robert Mellamphy, and each year on the last Saturday in May a Eucharist is celebrated in the church, followed by a procession to the site of the original shrine.

On 8th September, the nearest date to the original planned procession in 1529, a pilgrimage walk takes the same route as that intended by Thomas Wolsey from his college to the shrine.

The reciprocal Italian and English pilgrimages started at the time the shrine was restored in Ipswich, and have continued each year with increasing numbers, with school pupil exchanges beginning last year.

The essentially ecumenical nature of this revival has been most important, and in 2008 an Anglican/Catholic Dialogue began in Nettuno with papers presented by the Anglican Bishop of Whitby and Mgr Donald Bolen of the Pontifical Council for Promoting Christian Unity. These papers are reproduced in this book.

This article is by The Revd Haley Dossor, the former Priest-in-Charge of S. Mary at the Elms, Ipswich and is largely reproduced from *The Tablet* dated 14th June 2008.

Popular Devotion to the Blessed Virgin Mary in England – An Historical Perspective

IT MUST BE ASSUMED that the early development of Mariology and the expression of Marian Devotion in England was one with that of the whole of Christendom. As early as the 4th century S. John Chrysostom (d. AD 407), in a Eucharistic Prayer, refers to *'Mater Dei'* and this theology was later to be formalised by the definition of *Theotokos* at the Council of Ephesus in AD 431. This seems to be the first example of a repeating pattern in later times; popular devotion to Mary is followed by the emergence of established dogma formulated by the Church.

Following the Great Schism of 1054 and the separate development of the Eastern (later Eastern Orthodox) Church from that of the Western (later Roman Catholic) Church, development in the Church in England largely followed that of the Western Catholic tradition. However, the isolation of England from mainland Europe had long resulted in a considerable degree of independent development and expression in a number of areas of faith and practice. At the Synod of Whitby in AD 664 it was found necessary to align English Church structures and the Kalendar with the rest of the Church. In 1087 the Sarum Rite and Prayer Book was in use in England as a variation of the pre-Tridentine Rite used through the rest of Europe. It must be concluded as being highly likely that England showed similar independence in regard to Devotion to Our Lady.

This suggested independent development in Marian Devotion is supported by the founding of the Shrine of Our Lady of Walsingham in 1061. Marian Shrines dating from the 11th century are rare; most of those in Europe dating from the 13th to 15th centuries. Of significance is the fact that the Walsingham Shrine has its origin in documented Apparitions of Our Lady while the greater number of Shrines developed as a result of local cultus.

It may be said that what happened in Lourdes, France, in the middle of the 19th century, occurred in Walsingham, England, in the middle of the 11th century. In AD 1061 Our Lady appeared to the

Lady Richeldis at the remote Norfolk village of Little Walsingham. In this Apparition Our Lady instructed Richeldis to build a Holy House in honour of the Annunciation and that this House was to be a spiritual representation of the Nazareth Home of the Holy Family, "England's Nazareth". As a sign of Our Lady's grace and blessing a spring of water, forming a Holy Well was given. Miracles of healing were granted and Walsingham became a place of pilgrimage.

From its foundation, Walsingham rapidly grew in importance and as a place of popular pilgrimage; becoming among the foremost Shrines of Our Lady in Europe. This gave impetus for the development of popular devotion and the founding of numerous Marian shrines across the country. England became known as "Mary's Dowry" and it was said that those who travelled the "Walsingham Way", or Pilgrim routes, were as numerous as the "stars of the Milky Way in the heavens". Other important, though less famous, Marian Shrines include those at the old S. Paul's Cathedral in London; the Shrine of Our Lady of Pew at Westminster Abbey (significant because of the Royal status of the Abbey); Hempstead in Gloucestershire; Egmanton in Nottinghamshire; Fernyhalgh in Lancashire; Holystone in Northumberland and North Street, York, where a series of Apparitions of Our Lady is well documented.

Such became the extreme of development of Marian Devotion in England that, in the 13th century a Commission from Rome was charged with investigation and control of excess.

Major political, social and religious change occurred in England during the 16th century. The persecution of the Church in England under King Henry VIII and the iconoclasm and Reformations during the reigns of Edward VI and Elizabeth I largely brought to a close the public devotion to Mary and pilgrimage to Her shrines.

During this upheaval, many Images of Our Lady were removed or destroyed. The most notable images, including that of Our Lady of Walsingham and Our Lady of Grace, Ipswich, were taken to London for public burning. Some Images were rescued and escaped this destruction, notably that of *Maria Delle Grazie* of Nettuno. Private devotion, however, survived in England and the faithful secretly visited former shrines and holy places.

The 19th century Catholic Revival in the Church of England was complex and multi-stranded in its process and influence. However, in simple terms, it could be said to have been in two phases and to have had two resulting outcomes and expressions. The initial phase, begun in the University of Oxford between 1833 and 1841 (The Oxford Movement, The Tractarian Movement), was fundamentally academic and concerned with ecclesiology, liturgical theology and doctrine.

This initial phase emphasised that the Church of England embraced a continuity of authentic catholicity within its three-fold ordained ministry, ecclesial structure, sacramental theology, doctrine and spiritual expression. The later phase, during the late 19th and early 20th centuries, was manifested in Church social and political action, the development of Catholic worship, ritual, spirituality and devotion, including that relating to Our Lady. It was from this latter phase of the Catholic Revival that popular devotion to Our Lady regained full expression and has developed through to the present time.

The restoration of the Walsingham Pilgrimage in 1922 and the rebuilding of the Holy House from 1931 gave impetus to Marian Devotion, as did the restoration of the Shrine and Pilgrimage of Our Lady of Egmanton and other Shrines of more local popular devotion. The Lady Chapels that had survived in many Parish Churches found varying degrees of restoration.

This period also saw the foundation of a number of Catholic Societies giving support to both the clergy and the laity in their Christian and devotional life and ministry and to foster Vocations to ordained ministry and the religious life. Among them, the Society of the Holy Cross (*Societas Sanctæ Crucis*, SSC, founded 1855 for priests in the Catholic Tradition), the Confraternity of the Blessed Sacrament (CBS founded 1862 in honour of the Blessed Sacrament), the Church Union, the Federation of Catholic Priests, the Catholic League, the Guild of Servants of the Sanctuary, and the Additional Curates Society. A number of Religious Orders for men and women were founded.

The Society of Mary was founded in May 1931 from the amalgamation of two earlier Marian organisations: The

Confraternity of Our Lady (1880) and the League of Our Lady (1904). The work and influence of the Founder, Lord Halifax (Charles Lindley Wood, 1839-1934) gave great impetus and status. The Society has a Superior-General, a Chaplain-General, a Director of Pilgrimage and operates with an Executive and General Council. Local Wards are the focus for Members across Britain and internationally. In England, Marian Festivals are nationally organised in May and October and pilgrimage to shrines of Our Lady are fostered and arranged.

The Objects of the Society of Mary are: To love and honour Mary; To spread devotion to Her in reparation for past neglect and misunderstanding, and in the cause of Christian Unity; To take Mary as a model of purity, personal relationships and family life.

Though The Society of Mary is not associated with any one shrine of Our Lady, particularly strong relationships are enjoyed with Walsingham, where the Society maintains the Chapel of the Annunciation, and with Lourdes, where the Society has cordial relationships with the Bishop of Tarbes and Lourdes and the Shrine Authorities. Through the Nettuno-Ipswich friendship, the Society values the more recent association and friendship with the Shrines of Our Lady of Grace: S. Mary at the Elms, Ipswich, and that of *Maria Delle Grazie*, Nettuno.

Popular Devotion to Mary, fostered by the Society, will include the regular offering of Votive Masses of Our Lady, particularly on Saturdays, the praying of the Rosary of the Blessed Virgin Mary, the use of the Litanies of Our Lady, Novenas and prayers of intercession. The encouragement and support of Pilgrimage to shrines of Our Lady gives particular focus to devotional life and practice.

The devotional emphasis of the Society's work is supported by academic study. The important contribution to Marian Studies by Father John Milburn, sometime Chaplain-General of the Society, was recognised by the award of the Degree of Doctor in theology by the Pontifical Marian Academy.

In appreciating the place of popular devotion to our Lady in England it is necessary to understand that the Church of England, since the time of the Elizabethan Settlement in the mid-16th century, has been both Catholic and Reformed and encompasses a wide spectrum of traditions and expressions of the faith. Catholics in the Church of England emphasise the importance of reunion with the Holy See. Worship, spirituality and devotion are expressed in accord with Catholic tradition and practice. The ancient dogmas relating to Mary (eg. *Mater Dei, Semper Virgine*) are held, together with the more recent dogmas of the Assumption and Immaculate Conception.

In regard to Ecumenism, the Society of Mary can claim an historically significant history of engagement. Viscount Halifax initiated an ecumenical relationship with the Roman Catholic Church through the Malines Conversations 1921-1926. Through the close friendship, mutual respect and understanding between Lord Halifax and Joseph, Cardinal Mercier, an important beginning was made in Anglican-Roman Catholic dialogue.

In succession to this early initiative, the meeting between Pope Paul VI and Archbishop Michael Ramsey, and the subsequent dialogue, marked a milestone in ecumenical relationships. So too did the visit to Canterbury Cathedral of Pope John Paul II during the Archiepiscopate of Robert Runcie. The present expression of public relationship and respect between the Holy Father and Archbishop Rowan Williams, together with the nature of academic dialogue with the Holy See, gives continuing hope to all those seeking greater understanding and inter-relationships.

The recent publication of *Growing Together in Unity and Mission* charts the course of official Anglican-Roman Catholic dialogue over the past 40 years. The publication of the ARCIC II document *Mary: Grace and Hope in Christ* shows both the extent of the mutual and developing understanding of the role and place of Our Lady. It also charts remaining difficulties, revealing the necessity of continuing dialogue. This is especially the case with regard to the dogmas of the Assumption and of the Immaculate Conception. It is in this connection that it is relevant to take into account what was noted early in this Paper – that the official acceptance and formulation by the Church of Marian dogma has commonly followed after popular devotion is established. While Pope Sixtus IV instituted a Feast in honour of the Immaculate Conception in 1476, the Dogma was not promulgated until 1855 by Pius IX *(Ineffabilis Deus)*.

The Assumption was marked by Feasts from the 7th century, but the dogma was not promulgated until 1950 by Pius XII *(Munificentissimus Deus)*.

As a Devotional Society, the Society of Mary seeks to encourage an increase of devotional experience that will permit a continuing growth in understanding and acceptance of the Marian dogmas.

The Society of Mary, as emphasised in its Objects, sees Our Blessed Lady as having a most significant role in the cause for Christian Unity, relationship and re-union with the Holy See. The Society rejoices in the growing relationships developing through Lourdes, particularly during this 150th Jubilee Year. The Society has been charged by the Bishop of Tarbes and Lourdes to hold the "Mission for Ecumenism" among the 12 Missions of the Jubilee and the Superior General of the Society was privileged to join Bishop Perrier and Cardinal Ivan Dies in Opening the Jubilee Gates at Lourdes on the Feast of the Immaculate Conception on the 8th December 2007, at the inauguration of the Jubilee Year.

NB: The Lourdes Pilgrimage is covered in detail later in this book.

Thus, while important official and formal elements of ecumenical endeavour must continue, it is equally important that all who find inspiration in Mary, and look to Her in love and devotion, should continue to relate personally together in worship and celebration, in friendship and a growing mutual support and understanding.

May the prayers of Mary, our Mother and Sweet Queen, increase in us the love of God and the love between us, Her children.

✠ Robert, Whitby
May, 2008

This article was presented as a Paper at Nettuno by the Right Reverend Robert Ladds, Superior-General of The Society of Mary and formerly Bishop of Whitby.

Anglicans and Catholics
in dialogue about the Mother of God

IT IS A PLEASURE to be here in Nettuno today, and an honour to be a part of the programme at this holy place. My thanks to the Superior of the Shrine of Our Lady of Grace, Padre Giovanni Alberti, and to Signora Margherita Sonetto, for the invitation to be here today. It is also a delight to be present alongside Bishop Robert Ladds, who has come with other Anglican leaders and faithful, to be with us today.

In his fine presentation, the Bishop of Whitby has already made reference to the document *Mary: Grace and Hope in Christ*, produced by the Anglican-Roman Catholic International Commission (ARCIC) in 2005. Over the past 40 years, the official dialogue between the Anglican Communion and the Catholic Church has produced agreed statements on the Eucharist (1971), Ministry and Ordination (1973), Authority in the Church (1976, 1981, 1999), Salvation and Justification (1985), Ecclesiology (the nature of the Church (1990), Morals (1994), and most recently, on the place of Mary in the doctrine and life of the Church (2005). The Commission which prepared the Mary document was comprised of 18 bishops and theologians, half Anglican, appointed by the Anglican Communion office, and half Catholic, appointed by the Pontifical Council for promoting Christian Unity. *Mary: Grace and Hope in Christ* is the result of five years' work, and the sustained efforts of the Commission to address divisive issues about the place of Mary in the life and doctrine of the Church.

It is important to state at the outset that *Mary: Grace and Hope in Christ* is the work of ARCIC, but it is not at this point an authoritative declaration by the Catholic Church or by the Anglican Communion. It was, however, a unanimous statement, in which each bishop and theologian on the commission was willing to sign on to every line; so that is hopeful. The authorities who appointed the Commission have allowed the statement to be published so that it may be reflected upon and discussed and it is precisely on occasions like this, when Anglicans and Catholics gather together to celebrate Our Lady, that it is appropriate to reflect on ecumenical work which increasingly values the figure of Mary in our shared understanding. At the launch of the Mary document in Rome three years ago, Cardinal Kasper, President of the Pontifical Council for Promoting Christian Unity, noted that what is needed now is a wide-ranging reflection on the document itself, so that Anglicans and Catholics alike may feel drawn to conclude that the document "expresses our common faith".

The Mary document is distinct from the other subjects in the Anglican-Roman Catholic dialogue, in that it is not about something, but someone. It is about a person, Jesus' mother, the Mother of God Incarnate, one whose festivals we observe, one to whom we accord a special honour within the communion of the saints, one whom we recognise as "a model of holiness, obedience and faith for all Christians" (§2, citing Authority II, §30). All of this was in fact agreed between us before our work on this document started.

Before turning to the points of controversy which the document addressed – which had to do with Marian devotion, but principally to do with the Marian dogmas of the Immaculate Conception and the Assumption – I would like to begin by drawing out this 'personal' dimension by reflecting briefly on the Incarnation and the Annunciation, on the mystery which we touch upon when we reflect on Mary. Again, on these matters, there never has been a disagreement between Anglicans and Catholics, but it was important for the dialogue commission, and is important for us, to set out this foundational area of agreement before addressing the more difficult issues.

The Mary statement notes that Commission members were "convinced that any attempt to come to a reconciled understanding" of ongoing differences about Mary "must begin by listening to God's word in the Scriptures" (§77). The first section of the text, which is approximately a third of the Mary statement, offers an overview of the Scripture texts which speak of Mary. The text notes that "it is impossible to be faithful to Scripture and not to take Mary seriously", and that in studying the place of Mary within the Scriptures, "we have found ourselves meditating with wonder and gratitude on the whole sweep of salvation history: creation, election, the Incarnation, passion, and resurrection of Christ, the gift of the

Spirit in the Church, and the final vision of eternal life for all God's people in the new creation" (§6).

The Mary document also turned to the early Church, notably the patristic writings and the councils and creeds of the first five centuries, attentive to what they say about the place of Mary in salvation history. The Mary statement (§31-34) stresses the central importance of the early Church's understanding of Mary as the Mother of the Word Incarnate, as the 'God bearer' *(Theotókos)*. This title was given to Mary by the Christian teachers and councils of the fifth century to demonstrate the theological reality of the fact that her son, the historical Jesus, was God Incarnate. In this title, as in the Scriptures, Mary is always seen in relation to Christ. Reflection on Mary in the early Church was not an end in itself, but rather, a way of reflecting on Christ as fully human (born of Mary; §32) and fully divine (conceived by the Holy Spirit §33).

The mystery of a human being giving birth to God has long captured the Christian imagination, and this is reflected in Anglican writings as well as Catholic. Lancelot Andrews, an Anglican Bishop in the early 17th century, quotes the early church writer Eusebius speaking of how Mary, for nine months, *entertained within the closet of her flesh the hope of all the ends of the earth.* The Anglican poet John Donne grapples with the paradox of Mary as her *maker's maker;* she is the blessed one "whose womb was a strange heaven, for there God clothed himself, and grew…" A 15th century English hymn recently quoted in a Christmas message from the Archbishop of Canterbury speaks of Mary as the rose blossoming from the wintry earth of human history, and notes "for in this Rose contained was Heaven and earth in little space". The eternal Son of God, not contained by the whole universe, comes to dwell here, in the 'little space' of Mary's body.

S. Paul speaks about the treasure, the mystery hidden through the ages which has now been revealed to us in Christ. The mystery is God in our midst; the Master of the Universe, born as one of us. Mary carried the mystery within her very flesh, for nine months; she gave birth to the mystery, cradled the mystery. Mary carried in her arms Him who carries all creation. Anglicans and Catholics alike have long pondered this mystery, as Mary herself must have done.

We tried to express something of that in the document, and we also spoke in several places of the fundamental importance of Mary's openness to what was asked of her by God. The text returns repeatedly to Luke's account of the Annunciation, and in particular to Mary's *fiat:* "let it be done to me according to your word" (Luke 1:38). Her *fiat* is the "supreme instance" of a believer's embrace of God's will, a "free and unqualified consent in utter self-giving and trust" as she receives the Word "in her heart and in her body" (paras 5, 11). Her response to God's calling makes way for all that follows from it: "The Incarnation and all that it entailed, including the passion, death and resurrection of Christ and the birth of the Church, came about by way of Mary's freely uttered *fiat*" (para.5).

Building on that solid foundation, the Mary document proceeded to address areas which have historically been a source of division, not between all Anglicans, as we have just heard in the text of Bishop Robert, but between some Anglicans and the Catholic Church. Let me begin with the text's treatment of Marian devotion.

The text begins by speaking of how Anglicans and Catholics historically tended to think of Mary in different ways, but how this has shifted more recently: "Anglicans have tended to begin from reflection on the scriptural example of Mary as an inspiration and model for discipleship. Roman Catholics have given prominence to the ongoing ministry of Mary in the economy of grace and the communion of saints... Neither of these general characterisations do full justice to the richness and diversity of either tradition, and the twentieth century witnessed a particular growth in convergence as many Anglicans were drawn into a more active devotion to Mary, and Roman Catholics discovered afresh the scriptural roots of such devotion" (§65). The text then comes up with a strong common affirmation: "We together agree that in understanding Mary as the fullest human example of the life of grace, we are called to reflect on the lessons of her life recorded in Scripture and to join with her as one indeed not dead, but truly alive in Christ" (§65).

The Commission was then eager to make two points which aimed to assist Anglicans less familiar with Marian devotion. The first concerned intercession and mediation – the practice of believers asking Mary to intercede for them with her son – for instance in the

'Hail Mary'. The fear of some Anglicans historically has been that this practice threatened the unique mediation of Jesus Christ (§67). The Mary document cites the Second Vatican Council's Constitution on the Church, *Lumen Gentium* §60, saying that praying to Mary "no way obscures or diminishes the unique mediation of Christ, but rather shows its power". Assuring Anglican readers that we believe together that Jesus Christ is the one mediator between God and humankind, and rejecting any interpretation of the role of Mary which obscures this affirmation" (§68, citing the 1981 ARCIC document Authority II, §30), the text proceeds to stress that all ministries of the Church mediate the grace of God through human beings, and that Mary's very particular role in salvation history, as Mother of God, means that she "is believed to exercise a distinctive ministry of assisting others through her active prayer" (§71).

The second point concerning Marian devotion which the commission wanted to address touched on private revelation, especially Marian apparitions. Anglicans were encouraged by a statement of the Congregation for the Doctrine of the Faith from 2000, which stated that while private revelation "can be a genuine help in understanding the Gospel and living it better as a particular moment in time", it is a help which is offered, but which one is not obliged to use". The Congregation's statement continues "The criterion for the truth and value of private revelation is … its orientation to Christ himself. When it leads us away from him, when it becomes independent of him … then it certainly does not come from the Holy Spirit" (§73, citing the Congregation for the Doctrine of Faith, Theological Commentary on the Message of Fatima, 26th June, 2000).

In light of these clarifications, the Commission was able to conclude that "there is no continuing theological reason for ecclesial division" regarding Marian devotion (§75).

Finally, I would like to turn to the Catholic dogmas of the Immaculate Conception (1854) and Assumption of Mary (1950), since the major contribution of the Mary document lies here. Traditionally, Anglican theologians have questioned the Marian dogmas on two accounts: the papal authority by which they were defined, and whether they are sufficiently supported by Scripture.

The first question is a matter of authority, and was not addressed in this particular document. With regard to whether the content of the dogmas concerning Mary is supported by the Scriptures, the problematic is best formulated in relation to Article VI of the Anglican tradition's 39 articles. It states that the Scriptures contain all things necessary to salvation, and that the faithful should not be required to believe anything which is not in the Scriptures. It is clear from the outset that there is no direct reference to either the immaculate conception or the assumption of Mary, but what can be said about the relationship between these dogmas and the Scriptures?

ARCIC's argument in this regard is somewhat complicated, and I suggest that you read the document, but let me summarize quickly the core of what the text offers. Instead of focusing on any particular passage about Mary, the Commission began by noting that the Scriptures communicate something of a pattern of how the relationship between God and humanity should unfold, a pattern set down simply in S. Paul's letter to the Romans, where he writes: "We know that all things work together for good and for those who love God, who are called according to his purpose. For those whom he foreknew he also predestined to be conformed to the image of his Son… those whom God predestined he also called; those whom he called he also justified; and those whom he justified he also glorified" (Romans 8:28-30). This was the lens through which the Commission looked at Mary's vocation, and in particular, at the dogmas of the Immaculate Conception, which concerns Mary's preparation for her sacred calling at the very beginning of her life, and the Assumption which concerns its end.

The Roman text speaks of God knowing those he calls from the beginning of their existence – who are foreknown, predestined, called; that is whose lives are dynamized by God's grace from the start. This pattern is clearly seen in the life of Mary. She was "marked out from the beginning as the one chosen, called and graced by God through the Holy Spirit for the task that lay ahead of her" (§54). In Mary's freely uttered fiat – "let it be done to me according to your word" (Luke 1:38) – we see "the fruit of her prior preparation, signified in Gabriel's affirmation of her as 'graced'"

(§55). The Mary document is thus able to conclude:

> "In view of her vocation to be the mother of the Holy One (Luke 1:35), we can affirm together that Christ's redeeming work reached 'back' in Mary to the depths of her being and to her earliest beginnings. This is not contrary to the teaching of Scripture, and can only be understood in the light of Scripture. Roman Catholics can recognize in this what is affirmed by the dogma – namely 'preserved from all stain of original sin' and 'from the first moment of her conception'" (§59).

In turn, the document proposes that just as grace was operative at the beginning of Mary's life, it is also the case that there are Scriptural reasons for affirming that at the end of her life Mary was 'glorified', drawn fully into God's presence, and that this is consistent with a scriptural pattern. At the end of his life, Elijah was taken up by a whirlwind to heaven; Stephen sees the glory of God at the moment of his death; indeed the penitent thief is promised that he will soon be with Christ in paradise (2 Kings 2:11, Acts 7:54-60, Luke 23:43). These accounts "offer hints or partial analogies that may throw light on the mystery of Mary's entry into glory" (§56). While there is no direct testimony in Scripture concerning the end of her life, she is the one who bore God incarnate in her womb, who has a pre-eminent role among all of Jesus' disciples. Therefore "when Christians from East and West through the generations have pondered God's work in Mary, they have discerned in faith... that it is fitting that the Lord gathered her wholly to himself..." (§58). Again this allows the commission to conclude:

> "we can affirm together the teaching that God has taken the Blessed Virgin Mary in the fullness of her person into his glory as consonant with Scripture and that it can, indeed, only be understood in the light of Scripture. Roman Catholics can recognize that this teaching about Mary is contained in the dogma" (§58).

The Commission does not entirely resolve the differences between Anglicans and Catholics regarding the two dogmas, for the above conclusions do not address the authority by which they were defined. But it would indeed take us a long way forward on the road towards reconciliation.

Conclusion

In the Acts of the Apostles, S. Luke "notes that between the ascension of the Risen Lord and the feast of Pentecost the apostles were gathered in Jerusalem 'together with the women and Mary the mother of Jesus, and with his brothers' (Acts 1:14). Mary, who was receptive to the working of God's Spirit at the birth of the Messiah (Luke 1:35-38), is here part of the community of disciples waiting in prayer for the outpouring of the Spirit at the birth of the Church" (§21). As we celebrate this Feast of Pentecost, let us pray that the Spirit will lead Anglicans and Catholics ever more towards unity. Let us pray, and let us call forth Mary's intercession, for the Anglican Communion, and for the forthcoming Lambeth Conference, that the gifts of the Spirit may pour down upon all Anglicans and all who lead and serve their churches. And let us pray for all of us gathered here today, that with our Lady's assistance and inspired by her example, we might be ever open to the Holy Spirit and serve as instruments of the unity Christ desires for all his disciples.

This article was presented as a Paper at Nettuno by Mgr Donald Bolen, of the *Pontifical Council for promoting Christian Unity*.

Mary, hope of the one and only people of God

POPE PAUL VI, writing in 1974, in *Marialis Cultus* said 'Because of its ecclesial character devotion to the Blessed Virgin reflects the preoccupations of the Church herself. Among these, especially in our day, is her anxiety for the re-establishment of Christian Unity. In this way, devotion to the Mother of the Lord is in accord with the deep desires and aims of the ecumenical movement, that is, it acquires an ecumenical dimension'.

In earlier times, S. Augustine of Hippo said this to the faithful: 'How can you have nothing to do with Mary's childbearing if you are members of Christ's body? Mary gave birth to your head; the church gives birth to you. The Church is Mother and Virgin too, Mother in the bonds of love, Virgin in the fullness of faith and mercy. She brings her people to new birth as members of Christ whose body and bride she is. This is also why the Church is likened to the Virgin, since she brings many people to birth and unites them in Christ.' In another place he says, 'What Mary was privileged to keep in her body, the Church keeps in her heart; the distinction is that Mary gave birth to one Son, whereas the Church gives birth to many children, to gather them together into one, by means of that only Son of Mary.'

As Mother of the One (Christ as the head) and of the many (Christ as the body) and therefore of the one true God (head and body), the Mother of Christ is seen by the Church throughout the ages as a constant support for our unity in Christ, bringing into one the members of his body. So the Church is the Mother of Unity: therefore she has a duty to strive for the work of Ecumenism.

1. Ecumenical Marian events

As we celebrate every year the Week of Prayer for the Unity of Christians, Catholics venerate and call upon the Virgin as the sign and hope of that Unity. During our liturgies, ancient texts about the Mother of Christ are read which date from the time when the Church was united, not yet divided into East and West, Catholic, Protestant and Anglican. Among those theologians responsive to ecumenism and also among ordinary Christians who play an active part in the life of the Church, we often hear words like this: Mary of Nazareth is the woman with a heart closest to Christ, who breaks down the barriers which keep us apart.

We all hold in common that profession of the greatest Lutheran theologian of the 20th century, Karl Barth (d.1968) who in 1936 said of Mary: 'In her there is more than Abraham, more than David, more than John the Baptist, more than Paul and more than the whole Christian Church; this is the history of the Mother of God herself, a unique event which has no analogy'. (Dombes Group).

We rejoice in the news that Protestants, Muslims and Hindus will pray together at the Marian Shrine at Lourdes, the meeting place of people and nations. We understand that from September 22nd to 26th there will be a pilgrimage of Anglicans, Catholics and Protestants organised by the Society of Mary.

2. Ecumenical Marian Documents

Our dialogue about Our Lady springs from ecumenical studies and documents. I should like to draw your attention to four of them:

a. *The Dombes Group*

This association of French-speaking Catholic and Protestant theologians issued an important statement in 1998 through the Ecumenical monastic community of Bose, 'Mary in God's plan and in the Communion of Saints'. They conclude 'Our work has shown that nothing can allow Mary to become a symbol of what divides us. Elsewhere in the document they state 'It has to be remembered that Mary never has been a cause of separation between Churches. On the contrary, she has become a victim, an expression of our discontent. Quite different elements of division are focused and reflected upon her.'

Mary is the remnant onto whom each group of Christians projects its own prejudices against the other; she becomes in this way an innocent victim, a symbol of anti-Protestantism. This is how she has been used by both sides. This aspect of the conflict is now almost over at least at a theological level.

b. *The International Papal Marian Academy*

In their letter 'The Mother of Christ, our constant hope:

some issues about the person and the role of the Blessed Virgin Mary', when speaking about the Holy Spirit and the upper room, they say: 'Mary is the Mother of the unity which, amid a varied community of disciples, will soon help them to agree about prayer and to be noted for the 'brotherly union' of their members, a reconciling presence which is always with the Church on her pilgrim way.'

c. 'The only Mediator, the Saints and Mary' (1990) issued by the dialogue between Catholics and Lutherans in the United States

d. The joint statement from ARCIC II, 'Mary, Grace and Hope in Christ.'

In this document they affirm that 'Mary does not divide us' and conclude 'We believe that the issues concerning doctrine and devotion to Mary need no longer be seen as dividing communion nor an obstacle in a new stage of our growth into visible koinonia'. This text is based on what had already been achieved in previous stages of dialogue, particularly in "Authority and the Church" (1981) and "The Gift of Authority" (1999), finding in the scriptures an understanding of the place of Our Lady in the economy of Grace and of Hope (cf. Rom. 8.30). It includes a consideration of the papal dogmas of the Immaculate Conception and the Assumption and of the Catholic and Orthodox practice of asking the Mother of God and the Saints to pray for us. All this completes and surpasses what was achieved by the Dombes Group.

However, we cannot ignore the assertion of Paolo Ricci that 'Mary unites us but Mariology separates us' The *lex orandi* informs the *lex credendi*.

3. The *lex orandi, lex credendi*

The prophecy of Our Lady in the Magnificat is a prophecy of unity: 'All generations will call me blessed.' In spite of misunderstandings and differences about Mary, all believers praise her faith, imitate her hope and her love, give glory to her cooperation with the grace of the Holy Spirit and implore her motherly intercession for the Church and the world. Any historical, biblical and doctrinal reflection does not reveal any conflict in the understanding of the role of Mary within the Christian community even if theological and practical differences remain in the way in which it is expressed.

4. How is Our Lady in the Anglican Church seen by Catholics?

Paul VI asserts that 'Catholics are united with Anglicans, whose classical theologians have already drawn attention to the sound scriptural basis for devotion to the Mother of our Lord, while those of the present day increasingly underline the importance of Mary's place in the Christian life.' (M.C.32) We know very well that Anglicans recognise themselves as children of Mary, celebrate her feasts and have a close devotion to her. There is a vivid profession of this in the writings of John Baycroft, director of the Anglican Centre and the Archbishop of Canterbury's representative to the Holy See: "When I was a boy in the late forties", he writes in an article published in the monthly paper 'Jesus', "I left the Protestant Church of my childhood and joined the Anglican Church where I began to realise the importance of Mary. In my parish, the large painting over the altar where I used to pray represented the Virgin and Child. Each day at Evening Prayer, we sang the *Magnificat*. It was then that I discovered that the teaching of the Anglican Church was born from its liturgy – *lex orandi, lex credendi*. Mary is more important than anyone else except her Son. I found all her feasts in the Anglican Calendar except the Assumption. However, Anglicans were more moderate than Catholics in the way that faith was expressed. Devotionally and theologically, their attention was on the part she had played in the Incarnation: so she is *'Theótokos'*, the Mother of God, though there are no specific doctrinal definitions on this subject.

In 1950, I realised that Anglicans and Catholics could clash on Mary, when the dogma of the Assumption was proclaimed. Anglicans too believe that Mary is in heaven but do not try to establish the details of how she arrived there. This conflict is not to do with the place of Mary but how that should be expressed. Anglicans believe that a Council and not the Pope himself is the competent authority to define this teaching. Though details are not yet resolved about belief in the Assumption and the Immaculate Conception, the second half of the 20th century has seen a convergence between

Anglican and Catholic teaching. Since the mid-fifties, the Feast on August 15th begins to be recognised in Anglican Calendars together with other Marian feasts. Anglicans are particularly interested in Mary's role as the 'prototype' of a disciple, who shows us the future God intends for his Church; it sometimes appears that Pope John Paul II also is giving us an ecclesiology where Mary is more important than Peter. She is not only the Mother of God but also Mother of the Church, who prays for us and with us. By the grace of God, we too will share the glory of the resurrection of her Son.

In the Marian theology of the Anglican Communion, the Virgin, more so than Peter, is present in the Church. At the Annunciation, the Word becomes incarnate; in the visit to Elizabeth, the *Magnificat*, in Mary's prayers at Cana, at the foot of the Cross, in her unity with the Apostles on the Day of Pentecost, her vocation is demonstrated. Now the Feast of 15th August is celebrated in nearly all of the 37 districts of the Anglican Communion, and where it is not, the official Feast is 8th September. The Prayer Book of Papua New Guinea (1991) includes the texts of the 'Hail Mary, *'Angelus Domini'* and *'Regina Cæli'*. The Collect for the Falling Asleep of the Blessed Virgin Mary (August 15th) says: 'Lord, today we rejoice in the feast of Blessed Mary. She is the Model of your Church who responded to your call to bear Christ for the salvation of the world. May her prayers support us, so that we come to share with her the glory of your heavenly kingdom, where Jesus reigns with you and the Holy Spirit now and for ever.'

In the liturgy of the Church of England, there is a Preface for the Feasts of the Virgin Mary which says: 'And now we give you thanks because in choosing the Blessed Virgin to be the Mother of your Son, you have exalted the humble and meek. Your Angel greeted her as highly favoured; with all generations we call her Blessed and with her we rejoice and praise your holy name'.

5. What is the history of Marian devotion in the Anglican Church?
We acknowledge the following aspects of devotion in England:

a) According to Charles of Montalembert in his preface to the Life of S. Elizabeth, during the Pontificate of Innocent III (1216), William I of Scotland (died 1214) 'decided that the weekly rest from work had to start on a Saturday at noon, to give proof of his love for the Church and for the Holy Virgin'. This rest from work, the so-called 'English Saturday', though apparently created for humanitarian reasons during the feudal period, could have had its basis in Marian devotion, so that the working people would have more time to honour Mary.

b) Catholics asserted that S. Anselm of Aosta, Archbishop of Canterbury (died 1109), endorsed the clear tradition of Mary's having been conceived without Original Sin. However, Anselm plainly denies the Immaculate Conception, explaining that Christ, who did not inherit Adam's sin, is the only one without sin, while Mary, like all of us, descends from Adam. Nevertheless, Anselm accepts Mary as having been sanctified long before the birth of Jesus, thanks to the merits of her Son; he also accepts as an awe-inspiring idea the great goodness and holiness of the Virgin, being sanctified since she was in her mother's womb, as professed by famous teachers of that era (for example S. Bernard, Alexander of Hales Bonaventure, S. Albert the Great and S. Thomas Aquinas. Anselm implicitly confirms the Immaculate Conception, however, when he says, for example, 'It was fitting that the Virgin should be of such shining purity that none greater could be imagined other than God himself'. With this in mind, it may be noted that the English Church of those days acknowledged this truth about Mary, and was already celebrating a liturgical feast of the Conception of Mary: Anselm himself eventually re-established the Feast of the Immaculate Conception in England and at Lyons.

c) The Benedictine Eadmer of Canterbury (died 1124), a disciple of Anselm and a very humble monk who used to describe himself as 'an ordinary little man and a truly hardened sinner', is, for us, the first theologian and defender of the Immaculate Conception, before Duns Scotus. He reasons as follows: God *'potuit plane et voluit; si igitur voluit, fecit'* (obviously could do this and willed it; if therefore he willed it, he did it). He concludes with the benefits of this for the human race. Eadmer explains the Immaculate Conception by using the meaningful image of the chestnut, whose flawless fruit originates and develops in a pod, surrounded by thorns yet not being touched by their spines.

d) The Franciscan Duns Scotus was born between 23rd December 1265 and 17th March 1266. He taught in Oxford, Paris and Cologne, where he died on 8th November 1308 and where he is buried. He was beatified by Pope John Paul II on 20th March 1993, and he is known as 'Poet of the Word Incarnate and defender of the Immaculate Conception of Mary'. In the third book of his *'Ordinatio'*, Duns Scotus deals with the pre-redemption of the Virgin Mary, his axiom *'Potuit, decuit, ergo fecit'* being well known; *'potuit:* it was possible for God; *decuit:* it was fitting, on the basis of the principle of divine mercy; *fecit:* God did effect the Immaculate Conception'

e) The 'Oxford Movement' (also called the Tractarian Movement) which began around 1830, is always understood as wishing to defend the right of faith against the increasing claims of rationalism. This Movement also showed great attachment to the Mother of Christ.

f) It is known that Henry VIII, who died in 1547, died invoking the protection of the Virgin, in order to obtain eternal salvation.

g) We can refer currently to the book edited by F. Castelli entitled *Marian texts in the Second Millennium*, chapter 8, Literary texts, poetry and prose (published by Città Nuova, Rome 2002). Pages 437 to 530 deal with Mary in English Literature: before the year 1000 in the Anglo Saxon language known as Old English, in the 11th century at the time of the Norman Conquest, in the new vernacular of the 14th century. Marian devotion does not disappear after the schism in the Church in England: we have the poetry of John Donne (died 1631), a great poet and a believer. There is also interest in the Virgin in the Romantic and Victorian periods of the nineteenth century, and the Marian lyrics of the 20th century.

6. Concluding Remarks

a) The support from the 'lex orandi' and the interpretation of the 'lex credendi'

It is true that the 'Biblical Mary is for everybody', and that the Scriptures are the source and guide of faith common to all Christian denominations. However, this does not immediately resolve all questions, as some not inconsiderable disagreements remain with the problem of interpreting the Word. This is also due to different versions and to differing circumstances pertaining at any given time. Here the lex orandi helps the lex credendi. It is therefore necessary to reinstate the figure of the Virgin in the liturgy and in the daily prayers of the Churches. The Oxford Movement had as its aim to encourage the enrichment of the liturgical and devotional life of the Church of England. The restoration of the Shrine of Our Lady of Walsingham is much appreciated; here we venerate a statue of the Mother of God holding a sceptre, in a place of pilgrimage for Anglicans, Orthodox and Catholics.

b) More emphasis on Mary as woman of faith and Mother of believers

Pope John Paul II placed Mary, the believer, at the beginning of the New Covenant. If 'the faith of Abraham is the beginning of the Old Covenant, the faith of Mary at the Annunciation marks the beginning of the New Covenant'. Obedience to her faith pervades the whole existence of the Mother of Christ who becomes the Mother of all believers, alongside Abraham, 'our father in faith'.

This faith takes its origin in the Virgin Birth, since, as expressed by Augustine, 'Blessed Mary, the one who gave birth in faith, by faith conceived. In her 'heroic faith', we can 'find something like a key that opens up to us the inner reality of Mary'. She, who 'advanced in the pilgrimage of the faith' 'accomplishes in the most perfect way obedience to the faith'. She is the first among the witnesses to the faith, therefore a most excellent model of faith and love.

c) The 'Easter Motherhood' of Mary

Lutherans, especially in the past when talking of S. Paul, used to remind Catholics: 'From now on, therefore, we regard no one from a human point of view' (2 Cor 5:16). The body which Christ received from his Mother cannot be in possession of God's kingdom. For this reason, in order to see the continuity and the reciprocal relationships, sometimes Lutherans have laid stress on the distance between Jesus, Son of God and God himself, and Mary, who still remains a human creature.

However, we as Catholics maintain that just as the Incarnation of God's Word is ordained for his saving death (John 12:27-28), so Mary's divine motherhood is ordained for her 'Easter motherhood'. Beginning in Nazareth with her 'Behold the handmaid of the Lord' for the conception of the Redeemer, the collaboration of the Virgin in the Mystery of the Redemption reaches its culmination in Jerusalem, at the time of the crucifixion, where she 'suffered deeply with her only Son and joined with maternal love his sacrifice, lovingly accepting the immolation of the victim she begat'. Pope John Paul pointed out that 'her motherhood originated in Nazareth, and was lived to the full in Jerusalem, at the foot of the Cross'. Paul VI said previously that the maternal love of Mary towards Christ, 'grew wider, reaching a universal dimension at Calvary'

This 'new motherhood of Mary', generated by faith, is the fruit of the 'new' love which definitively reached its apex in her at the foot of the Cross, by means of her participation in the redeeming love of the Son. Augustine emphasised that Mary was the only woman to be at the same time mother and virgin, both in spirit and in body. However, 'spiritually she was not the mother of our Head, that is of our Redeemer, from whom rather she took her life... but is, without doubt, the mother of his limbs, that is us, in the sense that she was joined with love to the birth of believers of that Church, who are the limbs of that body. As far as her own body is concerned, she is the mother of the Head'.

Only one aspect of Mary as mother should be emphasised: as the mother of Christ as Head, in Bethlehem, and in Nazareth, and then of the whole of the human race at the Cross.

She is the mother of *'Christus totus'*, head and limbs. Jesus' head is to be considered together with the limbs of his body, starting with Mary and the Saints. The risen Lord is always accompanied by his servant and glorious Queen (Apoc 12:1; Ps 44:10-16), who by antonomasia [i.e. by her designation rather than her name], is part of the 'cloud of witnesses' of the faith (Hebrews 12:1).

As Mother of both the Head and the limbs, the Mother of God cannot divide the head from the body, Christ from the Church. If at the same time she is Mother of the limbs of the body of Christ, she is mother of the unity of the body of Christ. Consequently, she cannot ever divide the limbs she embraced in her suffering by the Cross.

So the Virgin can only encourage all believers with the exhortation; 'Do whatever he tells you.' (John 2:5).

Father Sergio Gaspari SSM
Centro Mariano Monfortano
000132 Colle Prenestino (Rome)

This article was presented by Father Sergio Gaspari SSM, at Nettuno in May, 2008.

Visit to the Pontifical Council
for Promoting Christian Unity

ON MONDAY 12th May the Pilgrims had the great privilege to visit The Vatican Office of the Pontifical Council for Promoting Christian Unity in Rome

On arrival we were again greeted by Mgr Donald Bolen. Mgr Bolen explained that this Office was founded as a direct outcome of the Second Vatican Council which had been convened by Pope John XXIII in 1962 and concluded after the fourth and final session in 1965. A most significant meeting took place in March 1963 when Archbishop Michael Ramsey visited Pope Paul VI. Three major developments came from this meeting: i) ARCIC; ii) An Anglican Office was founded in Rome; and iii) An exchange of rings between the Pope and the Archbishop took place. It emerged from the Council that there was clearly a need for such an office and some 25 people now work there. In the large room where major meetings are held and members of the Pilgrimage were privileged to meet, a beautiful Icon presented by the Orthodox Church of Ss Peter and Paul is displayed.

Mgr Bolen said a real Ecumenical difficulty would arise if a Schism occurs with the Church of England and it is difficult to envisage how discussions would progress. Nevertheless the search of Unity was not an easy thing, like a search for peace, but the Ipswich – Nettuno Pilgrimages were a great initiative and a help for ecumenism.

Anglican spirituality had a great deal to offer, but the Roman Communion would not be able to embrace the Anglican rite. Discussion towards unity would only be considered with the whole Anglican Communion, rather than any particular grouping within the Church.

The meeting concluded with prayers led by Cardinal Kasper.

Sermon preached by the Rt Revd Keith Newton
Bishop of Richborough
at S. Mary at the Elms, Ipswich

When the wine ran short, the mother of Jesus said to him, "They have no wine." And Jesus said to her, "Woman, how does your concern affect me? My hour has not yet come." His mother said to the servers, "Do whatever he tells you."

IF INDEED the statue of Our Lady of Grace in Nettuno is the one which was an object of piety here in Ipswich before 1538, then those who wanted to destroy it might be pretty perplexed by this afternoon's celebrations. Devotion to Our Lady over the last 500 years has often been a source of division and sadly for a small minority that is still true. But for many the study of Our Lady's unique place in the story of our salvation can draw Christians together from different traditions. The recent Report of the Anglican Roman Catholic International commission called *Mary: Grace and Hope in Christ* shows how much common ground there is between Catholics and many in the Anglican Church and not only those of us in the Catholic tradition in the Church of England.

This was underlined for me a few years ago when a Roman Catholic Abbot pointed out that at a time of falling congregations devotion to our Lady is increasing. This is because she points us to her son and draws us together in common devotion to him.

Isn't this what she has done here in Ipswich; Our common devotion to her has brought us together, not only from different denominations, but also different countries so that we may together learn to love the Lord Jesus, her precious son. Some of us recently have shared the annual celebration in Nettuno, and I loved that title coined by Don Carlo, the Parish Priest of *San Giovanni* in Nettuno, that she is the 'Star of Ecumenism.' Now we share this celebration today and on Monday we hope, God willing and weather permitting, to be together at Walsingham.

Today we celebrate that Mary shared in a unique way in co-operation with the redeemer and that she intercedes for us that we may live the life of grace which flows from her son.

Not all shrines of Our Lady are the same. The ethos is often different and the emphasis is different. Lourdes is particularly identified with the feast of the Immaculate Conception which focuses on the purity of Our Lady and God's preparation of her to be the instrument of the incarnation. The angel greeted her even before the invitation to co-operate with God with those words we use often 'Hail Mary Full of Grace'. She was already a graced woman when the angel greeted her. Not only was she free from sin but free to receive God's greatest gift, the gift of himself. She is described by William Wordsworth as 'our tainted nature's solitary boast', chosen by God at her conception for the part she would play in the story of our salvation.

Walsingham, on the other hand a particularly English Shrine, is a homely place – England's Nazareth,– which speaks to us of the Holy Family and their home in Nazareth before the public ministry of Jesus.

Home, we say is where the heart is. We know what makes a home is far more is more than bricks and mortar and mere possessions. It is a place of security, where we feel at ease; a place of comfort, security and love. We know almost nothing of those early years in Nazareth except for the brief story of the finding in the Temple in S. Luke's Gospel.

What we see in the Holy Family and the interaction of Jesus, Mary and Joseph is the context in which we too can grow to full maturity. Nazareth provides us with a model. In a world where human relationships are often threatened or broken, where loving families, in some parts of the country, are the exception, there is the challenge to hear the gospel and live it in our homes, that is after all where charity, true love begins.

The German theologian Dietrich Bonhoeffer wrote:

> "Most people have forgotten nowadays what a home can mean, though some of us have come to realise it as never before. It is a kingdom of its own in the midst of the world, a haven of refuge amid the turmoil of our age, nay more a sanctuary. It is not founded on the shifting sands of private and public life but has its peace in God. For it is God who gave it its special meaning and dignity, its nature and privilege, its destiny and

worth. It is an ordinance God has established in the world, the place where peace, quietness, joy love, purity, continence, respect, obedience, tradition and to crown them all, happiness may dwell, whatever may pass away in the world".

Sadly we are bombarded day after day with unrealistic and unattainable dreams. My son had a record a few years ago where over the music someone said 'never read beauty magazines they only make you feel ugly'. The same might be said for home magazines they only make yours look dowdy. But they are really about houses not about the essence of homes.

God entrusted Jesus to the care of Mary and Joseph and he entrusts our families too, whether children and parents or just friends and relatives. We cannot know our future any more than Mary knew or understood what it would be for Jesus. As Mary did, we need to store up and ponder events in our lives, striving to achieve the quality of her love in Nazareth not so very different from ours, full of joys and sorrows. We are to be like her trusting all to God with the quiet love of the saviour.

But we know how hard it is, we need God's grace to help us to do it. We cannot achieve this in our own strength. To aid us to build the Church and our lives on the foundations of his love he has given us the person of Mary his mother not simply to be an example but also a help: Mary help of Christians: Our Lady of Grace. He gave her to S. John at the foot of the cross that we, too, with him, might take her to our homes as mother.

Today's gospel tells us of the first miracle at Cana. We see there she has two roles. Firstly she makes known to Jesus the needs of the community. She sees the needs of the wedding reception even before others do and turns to Jesus 'They have no wine'. She is first and foremost the servant the handmaid. She knows the needs of the world and the Church and she intercedes for us. Indeed this miracle reflects her role as an intercessor for us with all the saints. She is in the middle, a mediator in the story beseeching her son for the needs of the world 'Holy Mary Mother of God pray for us sinners now and at the hour of our death'. We think of her in constant prayer for us that his kingdom may come in its fullness.

But secondly she knows the only way to fullness of life, to be brimming full with the wine of faith and love, is to do what Jesus tells us to be faithful and obedient to him: 'Whatever he says do it.'

The second reading from Acts shows Mary in prayer with the apostles before Pentecost so we need to pray through and with Mary for the Unity of the Church.

We can learn so much from Our Lady but she never usurps her son. In discovering more about Mary, we are drawn deeper into the mystery of the incarnation and our redemption and deeper into communion with each other as fellow members of the Body of Christ.

Evviva Maria

The Pilgrimage to Lourdes
sponsored by The Society of Mary and The Shrine of Our Lady of Walsingham

Introduction

AMONG THE MANY Marian Shrines in Europe, Lourdes is the foremost. The year 2008 was the 150th anniversary of the first apparition of Our Lady to Bernadette in a grotto on the hillside of Massabielle, near Lourdes, a small insignificant town in southern France. For it was on that blustery day of 11th February 1858 that Mary appeared in a shallow cave on the bank of the river Gave and looked with love at Bernadette Soubirous, a diminutive teenager. Mary made a large sign of the cross, which unfroze Bernadette and then together they prayed the Rosary. Our Lady's message to the world unfolded with seventeen more apparitions being passed on to her chosen messenger, reaching at its peak on 25th March when Mary said: "I am the Immaculate Conception".

Several requests were made by Our Lady to Bernadette, including: i) "You will pray for sinners"; ii) "Go drink at the spring and wash in it", iii) For processions to come to Massabielle, and iv) For a chapel to be built.

For some years Bernadette suffered greatly from the suspicious disbelief of some and the tactless enthusiasm and insensitive attention of others. In 1866 Bernadette was admitted to the convent of the Sisters of Charity at Nevers, where she was more sheltered from trying publicity, but not from the 'stuffiness' of the convent superiors nor from the tightening grip of asthma. 'I am getting on with my job' she would say. What is that someone asked? 'Being ill', was the reply and she continued to live her self-effacing life, dying at the age of only thirty-five.

The events of 1858 have resulted in one of the greatest pilgrim shrines in the history of Christendom. But S. Bernadette took no part in the developments, nor was it for her visions that she was canonised, but for the humble simplicity and religious trusting-ness that characterized her life.

One of the Objects of The Society of Mary, as listed in the Manual and, as referred to, in Bishop Robert Ladds paper presented in Nettuno is:-

> *"To spread devotion to her in reparation for past neglect and misunderstanding, and in the cause of Christian Unity."*

Bishop Perrier, of Tarbes and Lourdes, selected twelve themes to be observed by Lourdes throughout the Jubilee Year. It was so thoughtful and appropriate that the one he assigned to The Society of Mary was Mission for Christian Unity.

The Society of Mary and The Shrine of Our Lady of Walsingham jointly arranged the special Pilgrimage to Lourdes in 2008 which was deliberately timed to coincide with the feast of Our Lady of Walsingham. By the invitation of Bishop Perrier both The Archbishop of Canterbury and Cardinal Kasper, the President of the Congregation for the Promotion of the Unity of Christians, were present on Tuesday evening and throughout Wednesday. Following the Rosary Torchlight Procession on Tuesday evening they jointly Solemnly proclaimed the Feast of Our Lady of Walsingham. At the Mass in the Basilica of S. Pius X on the following morning Cardinal Kasper was the Principal Celebrant and The Archbishop preached, whilst in the afternoon they presented papers at an Ecumenical

Conference. The Archbishop also Officiated at both the Liturgy of Reconciliation and Benediction on Thursday morning, followed by a final group visit to the Grotto, *at which he gave a moving homily in that most sacred spot,* and concluded with the presentation of the Pilgrim Candle especially for the intention of Unity.

Over 400 people joined the Pilgrimage, including 9 Bishops and 75 Priests.

Sermon by
the Most Reverend Rowan Williams
Archbishop of Canterbury
at the International Mass in the Basilica of S. Pius X

'The babe in my womb leaped for joy.' (Luke 1:44)

MARY comes to visit Elizabeth, carrying Jesus in her womb. The Son of God is still invisible – not yet born, not even known about by Elizabeth; yet Elizabeth recognises Mary as bearing within her the hope and desire of all nations, and life stirs in the deep places of her own body. The one who will prepare the way for Jesus, John the Baptist, moves as if to greet the hope that is coming, even though it cannot yet be seen.

Mary appears to us here as the first missionary, 'the first messenger of the gospel' as Bishop Perrier of Lourdes has called her: the first human being to bring the good news of Jesus Christ to another; and she does it simply by carrying Christ within her. She reminds us that mission begins not in delivering a message in words but in the journey towards another person with Jesus in your heart. She testifies to the primary importance of simply carrying Jesus, even before there are words or deeds to show him and explain him. This story of Mary's visit to Elizabeth is in many ways a very strange one; it's not about the communication of rational information from one speaker to another, but a primitive current of spiritual electricity running from the unborn Christ to the unborn Baptist. But mission it undoubtedly is, because it evokes recognition and joy.

Something happens that prepares the way for all the words that will be spoken and the deeds that will be done. The believer comes with Christ dwelling in them by faith, and God makes that current come alive, and a response begins, not yet in words or commitments, but simply in recognising that here is life.

When Mary came to Bernadette, she came at first as an anonymous figure, a beautiful lady, a mysterious 'thing', not yet identified as the Lord's spotless Mother. And Bernadette – uneducated, uninstructed in doctrine – leapt with joy, recognising that here was life, here was healing. Remember those accounts of her which speak of her graceful, gliding movements at the Lady's bidding; as if she, like John in Elizabeth's womb, begins to dance to the music of the Incarnate Word who is carried by his Mother. Only bit by bit does Bernadette find the words to let the world know; only bit by bit, we might say, does she discover how to listen to the Lady and echo what she has to tell us.

So there is good news for all of us who seek to follow Jesus' summons to mission in his Name; and good news too for all who find their efforts slow and apparently futile, and for all who still can't find their way to the 'right' words and the open commitment. Our first and overarching task is to carry Jesus, gratefully and faithfully, with us in all our doings: like St Teresa of Avila, we might do this quite prosaically by having with us always a little picture or a cross in our pockets, so that we constantly 'touch base' with the Lord. We can do it by following the guidance of the Orthodox spiritual tradition and repeating silently the Jesus Prayer, 'Lord Jesus Christ, Son of God have mercy on me, a sinner'. And if we are faithful in thus carrying Christ with us, something will happen, some current will stir and those we are with will feel, perhaps well below the conscious surface, a movement of life and joy which they may not understand at all. And we may never see it or know about it; people may not even connect it with us, yet it will be there – because Jesus speaks always to what is buried in the heart of men and women, the destiny they were made for. Whether they know it or not, there is that within them which is turned towards him. Keep on carrying Jesus and don't despair: mission will happen, in spite of all, because God in Christ has begun his journey into the heart.

And when we encounter those who say they would 'like to believe' but can't, who wonder how they will ever find their way to a commitment that seems both frightening and hard to understand, we may have something to say to them too: 'Don't give up; try and hold on to the moments of deep and mysterious joy; wait patiently for something to come to birth in you.' It certainly isn't for us as Christians to bully and cajole, and to try and force people into commitments they are not ready to make – but we can and should seek to be there, carrying Jesus, and letting his joy come through, waiting for the leap of recognition in someone's heart.

Of course, as often as not, we ourselves are the one who need to hear the good news; we need people around us who carry Jesus, because we who call ourselves believers all have our moments of confusion and loss of direction. Others fail us or hurt us; the Church itself may seem confused or weak or even unloving, and we don't feel we are being nourished as we need, and directed as we should be. Yet this story of Mary and Elizabeth tells us that the Incarnate Word of God is always already on the way to us, hidden in voices and faces and bodies familiar and unfamiliar. Silently, Jesus is constantly at work, and he is seeking out what is deepest in us, to touch the heart of our joy and hope.

Perhaps when we feel lost and disillusioned, he is gently drawing us away from a joy or a hope that is only human, limited to what we can cope with or what we think on the surface of our minds that we want. Perhaps it's part of a journey towards his truth, not just ours. We too need to look and listen for the moments of recognition and the leap of joy deep within. It may be when we encounter a person in whom we sense that the words we rather half-heartedly use about God are a living and actual reality. (That's why the lives of the saints, ancient and modern, matter so much) It may be when a moment of stillness or wonder suddenly overtakes us in the middle of a familiar liturgy that we think we know backwards, and we have for a second the feeling that this is the clue to everything – if only we could put it into words. It may be when we come to a holy place, soaked in the hopes and prayers of millions, and suddenly see that, whatever we as individuals may be thinking or feeling, some great reality is moving all around and beneath and within us, whether we grasp it or not. These are our 'Elizabeth' moments – when life stirs inside, heralding some future with Christ that we can't yet get our minds around.

It's very tempting to think of mission as something to be done in the same way we do – or try to do – so much else, with everything depending on planning and assessments of how we're doing, and whether the results are coming out right. For that matter, it's tempting to think of the Church's whole life in these sorts of terms. Of course we need to use our intelligence, we need to be able to tell the difference between good and bad outcomes, we need to marshal all the skill and enthusiasm we can when we respond to God's call to share his work of transforming the world through Jesus and his Spirit. But Mary's mission tells us that there is always a deeper dimension, grounded in the Christ who is at work unknown and silent, reaching out to the deeply buried heart of each person and making the connection; living faithfully at the heart of the Church itself, in the middle of its disasters and betrayals and confusions, still giving himself without reserve. All that we call 'our' mission depends on this; and if we are wise, we know that we are always going to be surprised by the echoes and connections that come to life where we are not expecting it.

True mission is ready to be surprised by God – 'surprised by joy', in the lovely phrase of C. S. Lewis. Elizabeth knew the whole history of Israel and how it was preparing the way for God to come and visit his people – but she was still surprised into newness of life and understanding when the child leapt in her womb. Bernardette's neighbours and teachers and parish clergy knew all they thought they needed to know about the Mother of God – and they needed to be surprised by this inarticulate, powerless, marginal teenager who had leapt up in the joy of recognition to meet Mary as her mother, her sister, bearer of her Lord and Redeemer. Our prayer here must be that, renewed and surprised in this holy place, we may be given the overshadowing strength of the Spirit to carry Jesus wherever we go, in the hope that joy will leap from heart to heart in all our human encounters; and that we may also be given courage to look and listen for that joy in our own depths when the clarity of the good news seems far away and the sky is cloudy.

But here today, with Elizabeth and Bernardette, we say, in thankful amazement, 'Why am I so favoured, that the mother of my Lord should come to me?' And we recognise that our heart's desire is met and the very depth of our being stirred into new life.

© Rowan Williams
September, 2008

Ecumenical Conference
'Mary and the Unity of the Church'

Ecumenical Dialogue, Wednesday 24th September, 2008

Hosted by Bishop Jacques Perrier of Tarbes and Lourdes, during Archbishop Williams' Pilgrimage to the Shrine of Our Lady of Lourdes.

Paper presented by Cardinal Walter Kasper
President of the Pontifical Council for Promoting Christian Unity

I EXTEND my warm greeting to you all, and also a heartfelt greeting from the Holy Father, who was here in Lourdes only some days ago. A greeting to the Archbishop of Canterbury and the bishops with him, to the Catholic bishops and not least to the Bishop of Tarbes-Lourdes, who has so hospitably received us.

Lourdes is known for its miracles; today we too are witnesses of a miracle of a particular sort. Who could have imagined only twenty or thirty years ago that – as is happening today – Catholic and Anglican pilgrims would undertake together a pilgrimage from the National Shrine of Our Lady in Walsingham in Great Britain to this internationally recognised site of Marian pilgrimage for the celebration of the 150th anniversary of the apparitions of Our Lady, and that on this occasion a Roman Catholic Cardinal and the Archbishop of Canterbury, head of the Anglican Communion, together with seven other Anglican bishops, would worship together? For those who are aware of the disputes and the polemics of the past about Mary between Catholics and Christians from non-

Catholic Churches, for those who know of the reserves in the non-Catholic world towards Marian pilgrim sites such as Lourdes, for all these people this unprecedented event today is a kind of miracle.

Yes, indeed, we could even say that the whole ecumenical movement could be classified among miracles. After centuries of division and often of enmity between Christians of many denominations, our modern times have marked the beginning of a common pilgrimage towards the unity that Jesus prayed for on the eve of his death, when he asked His Father that all his disciples may be one. The Second Vatican Council was right when it affirmed that the ecumenical movement is not a merely human enterprise and effort, but an impulse of the Holy Spirit to fulfil Jesus' testament at the end of his earthly life. So since the Second Vatican Council the Church is in mission for the unity of all Christians, as you highlight by your pilgrimage, and I congratulate you for this wonderful idea.

So let us reflect this afternoon on a theme which is not a usual or obvious one among ecumenists, but which is nevertheless an important one. Let us talk about Mary and the unity of the Church, Mary and the ecumenical movement towards full visible unity.

I.

This is not such a hopeless issue as some may think. There has been Marian devotion in all periods of Church history, as Our Lady herself prophesied: 'From now on all generations will call me blessed!' As Catholics we share the veneration of Our Lady especially with our Orthodox brothers and sisters, who praise her in many wonderful hymns as the *Theótokos* (Mother of God), the *Aeiparthenos* (Ever virgin) and the *Panhagia* (the All-holy).

But there was Marian devotion also at the time of the Reformation. Martin Luther in 1521 wrote a wonderful and admirable text on Mary's famous canticle, the Magnificat, a text which only 17 years later was published also in English. Luther remained all his life a fervent venerator of Mary, whom he confessed with the ancient Creeds and Councils of the undivided Church of the first millennium as virgin and Mother of God. He was critical only about some practices, which he believed to be misuses and exaggerations. There are also many other texts from the Reformers of the 16th century, which in the last century were collected and published under the title *Das Marienlob der Reformatoren* [Mary's praise by the Reformers, 1987].

In the English Reformation of the 16th century we find the same phenomenon. Though the medieval Shrine of Our Lady of Walsingham, dating from the 11th century, was sadly destroyed by order of King Henry VIII, the English Reformers themselves continued to receive the doctrine of the ancient church concerning Mary – Mary as ever virgin, as Mother of God – because they considered these doctrines both scriptural and in accord with ancient common tradition. So the Anglican Common Prayer Book of the 16th century maintained the traditional Marian feasts during the liturgical year: Conception of Mary; Nativity of Mary; Annunciation; Visitation and Purification/Presentation.

But sadly – especially since the time of the Enlightenment – there has mainly prevailed a spirit known as mariological minimalism in Protestant and also in some Anglican circles. Our Lady was often neglected and the biblical witnesses about her overlooked; some have even believed that they have to complete the Reformation by rejecting what the Reformers still maintained from the ancient and common tradition.

In our times through a renewed and fresh reading and meditation of the Holy Scriptures we see a slow but decisive shift. There are today not a few Evangelical and Anglican women who discover Mary as their sister in faith. In the official German Evangelical Catechism for Adults published exactly 20 years ago in 1988 one finds the interesting and to some extent surprising affirmation: 'Mary is not only 'catholic'; she is also 'evangelical''. She is evangelical because she occurs in the Evangelium, in the Gospel. A further Lutheran-Catholic statement *Communio sanctorum* [Communion of Saints] (2000) and a statement of the famous Group of Dombes in France, Mary in God's Salvation Plan and in the Communion of Saints (1997), deepened this view and brought further progress in a common understanding and believing.

Finally, of special importance in our context there is the latest document, an agreed statement, of our common Anglican/Roman Catholic International Commission (ARCIC), issued in 2004, which bears the significant title *Mary: Grace and Hope in Christ*. While this agreed statement did not reach full consensus, there was an unexpected very high degree of consensus about the special place of Mary in salvation history, in the life of the Church and in Christian discipleship.

This short account of our ecumenical dialogues tells us: Mary is not absent, she is present in the ecumenical dialogues; the churches have made progress in rapprochement about the doctrine on Our Lady. Our Lady is no longer dividing us, she is reconciling and uniting us in Christ her son. Especially the result of our Anglican/Roman Catholic dialogue, in the midst of some sad turbulences and disappointments in other fields in our relations, we can nonetheless see as a positive and encouraging hopeful sign, perhaps even almost a small miracle, for which gift we cannot be grateful enough to the Lord. There is reason for hope, that Our Lady will help us to overcome the present difficulties in our relations so that with God's help we can continue our common ecumenical pilgrimage, which we started by the impulse of God's Spirit and which up to now has been blessed with so many good fruits. I am really convinced: as has happened often in the past, Mary will also in our times and in the future be the helper of Christianity in situations of need, as we experience today in our ecumenical pilgrimage.

II.

In what follows I do not intend to give a full account of all the above-mentioned documents, and even less a full account of the whole theological debate on the doctrine on Mary in the present ecumenical context. Here I want to deal with the theme 'Mary and the Unity of the Church' only from a Catholic perspective, and I can do this only in a fragmentary way. But I will take some inspiration from the title of the above mentioned Anglican/Catholic agreed statement *Mary: Grace and Hope in Christ*. For this title tells us that Mary is a unique sign and a unique witness of what is the centre and the heart of the Good News of the Gospel; she is a unique sign and a unique witness of what is central in Christian discipleship; finally she stands for what we today lack and what we need the most: grace and hope – grace and hope also on the way to the unity of the Church: grace and hope.

First, grace. The evangelist Luke in the beginning of his Gospel tells about the annunciation of the coming of the Son of God in the flesh of our world. The angel greets the virgin Mary, 'Hail Mary, full of grace, the Lord is with you'. In the Greek text we read, Hail Mary, *kecharismene,* which in English is often translated as 'You are favoured', i.e., God has a special eye for you, he has favoured and elected you from all eternity, he has blessed you and prepared you with the fullness of his grace in order that you without any stain of sin would be prepared for your unique vocation and your unique mission to become the mother of the Lord, the Son of God and the Saviour of all mankind. With you, the salvation of the world enters its final step; you, full of grace, are the dawn of the new mankind, of the new creation.

To look at Mary means to cast our minds on eternity and to see the eternal plan of God for the salvation of mankind and to know God's abundant grace by which He did not want that after the fall into sin and all its tragic consequences, the alienation between men and women, between the different ethnic groups, the alienation within us which followed from the alienation from God, He did not want that we should be lost for ever. It is only by God's Yes to us and to the world, it is only by His grace that mankind can survive.

In this eternal plan of salvation Mary has her place and her mission. She stood at this moment of the annunciation vicariously for the whole of mankind. By her Yes, 'Yes, here I am; I am the servant, the handmaid of the Lord', by this her Yes the eternal Yes of God could take place in our world. She spoke this humble Yes on behalf of us all, on behalf of all mankind. But she did it not for herself, as she did nothing for herself, she did it as the kecharismene, as blessed and as full of grace. So she could magnify God: 'Tell out, my soul, the greatness of the Lord; rejoice, rejoice, my spirit in God my saviour.'

Thus, Mary is sign, witness, prophet and receiver of God's grace. She tells us: Nothing is possible, nothing can be done, neither we nor the whole world could survive, without God's grace. For all we are, we have to thank God; for all, we have to praise God, our creator and our redeemer. We too have to rejoice for his gracious Yes, which He speaks to every one of us. We exist also only by grace. In each moment of our life God has to say to us: Yes, I want you to be. And above this, we are saved not by our modest merits and efforts, not by our more or less decent moral behaviour or our human deeds, but only by grace, *sola gratia*. In this fundamental truth Catholics, Anglicans and Protestants no longer have any controversies; in this fundamental truth they can witness and proclaim together to a world which needs this message, because it is wrong when it thinks that with our scientific and technical skills we ourselves can manage our happiness. No, we are not the makers of our own happiness. We live and we are saved out of grace.

What is true regarding every one of us, is true also for the whole community of believers, for the Church. The Church is not only a socially constructed body, not merely the result of human willingness to live, to work and to be together. If the Church were to have survived only from her human potentialities, she would have collapsed long ago. No, the Church exists and lives because she, represented by Mary, is the *kecharismene*, the favoured, the elected, convoked, blessed and filled with grace by the Lord. As Church we are God's people and his temple.

Therefore, we cannot 'make', organise or manipulate the unity of the Church. The full unity for which we look and pray is - as is all salvation history - God's work, God's gift and God's grace. The very heart and core of ecumenism is therefore spiritual ecumenism, which makes ours the prayer of our Lord on the eve of his passion: 'That all may be one'.

The great master of spiritual ecumenism, the French *Abbé* Paul Couturier, formulated the goal of the ecumenical movement not as a unity understood as our project but a unity when, where and how God wants it to be. Ecumenism is not a matter of our projects. It is God's project. We are not the masters of this process. But we know that whoever prays in the name of Christ can be sure that their prayer will be granted. To make ours the prayer of Christ for the unity of his disciples holds the promise that unity will come – when, where and how God's sovereign providence has disposed.

III.

This brings me to the next point. Mary – as we said – is a sign and a witness of God's Yes to our world, to every one of us and to the Church. But now we must complete this first thesis with a second one. Mary answered to God's Yes with her Yes. 'Here I am; I am the servant, the handmaid of the Lord.' So as the Mother of God she became the entrance of God in our world. She donated Jesus Christ to us and to all mankind. But motherhood does not end with giving birth to a child; a mother remains a mother forever. So Our Lady accompanied with her motherhood the whole existence of her son till the end of his earthly life. With sorrow she searched for him when as a twelve year-old he seemed to be lost, and she followed him till the cross. She stood under the cross suffering with him and adding her suffering to his own, becoming the mother of sorrows. She stood not only physically under the cross, for with her stood the Yes she spoke in the beginning. She remained faithful to her vocation and her mission.

Also under this aspect Mary is an example, a model, a type of our discipleship. God wants our Yes in response to his Yes; God wants us to be – inspired, sustained and empowered by his grace – co-workers and co-operators in his salvific work. Or as Saint Augustine put it: 'He who has created us without us, does not redeem us without us.' Every one of us has his or her personal vocation and mission, his or her personal charisma, everybody has his or her place. These are not always and normally are not great, generally noticed, powerful, spectacular vocations and missions. Mary does not stand for the mighty, the haughty and the rich; she stands for the little ones, the powerless, the poor, the meek, the humble. She is tender with the sick and the disabled, tender also with the sinners. All these are children of God. So every one of us has his or her task, his or her momentum in the world and in the Church for the realisation of God's plan of salvation.

Each of us has also the mission to work for the realisation of Christ's last will, the unity of his disciples. There are many ways to cooperate, more than we normally think: by prayer as we have already said, by suffering, by a life of purity and holiness, by dialogue of life and love, by interest and respect for the faith of other

Christians, by solidarity also with the internal problems of other Christian communities, as brothers and sisters in Christ we should help each other; then we can cooperate by giving witness of our Catholic faith and by patiently and with love explaining our position, when others have difficulty in understanding it; so we can learn from one other, what Pope John Paul II called an exchange not only of ideas but of gifts. In all of this we should not forget: unity can be brought about by love and by truth. Both are intimately linked. Truth without love can be harsh and repelling; but love without truth becomes dishonest; so we should tell the truth in love, i.e., not with arrogance but with respect, sensitivity and patience.

Finally we can and we should give witness together on what we have in common, which is much more than what divides us. Our modern world needs our common witness. And when we speak in common our voice will be much more convincing. So wherever possible we should speak with one voice and should work together for the coming of God's reign in our world.

IV.

Let me now come to a last point, and perhaps the most important point. We started with the annunciation, the beginning of our Lady's mission. Now we turn to the end of Jesus' earthly life: Mary under the cross. From the cross Jesus saw his mother and the disciple whom he loved standing beside her, and spoke the famous words: 'Mother, here is your son', and to the disciple: 'Here is your mother'.

The disciple whom Jesus loved is in the fourth Gospel the representative of all disciples. He stands for us all. So Jesus, when he left this world, did not want to leave us as orphans. He left us his mother as mother of us all. He made her in a certain and correctly understood sense mother of the Church. And as normally every mother is the centre of unity in a family, so also our Lady was made mother of the unity of the Church.

First – as the Second Vatican Council with reference to a saying of Saint Ambrose told us – she is typos, type of Church unity. She – the first of all disciples of Christ – represents what the Church is or should be: the faithful undivided Yes to God's Yes in a life of purity and holiness, a life of prayer and love. She tells us what to do. At the wedding of Cana-in-Galilee she told the servants: 'Do whatever He tells you!' She does not point to herself, she points to Jesus!

For what other reasons have there been and still are for the divisions in the Church, than that we have not and still do not live as Jesus tells us, than that our love and our faith have been weakened. There are growing rifts also today, because many do not listen to what Jesus and the Holy Scriptures tell us, but what in modern and post-modern culture seems to be pleasant. Always when worldly thinking and measures of this world make inroads into the Church, then the unity of the Church is at risk. Mary guides us not to what pleases everybody, but she guides us sometimes also under the cross. So there is no other means to retrace our way back to full unity than to be, as Mary was, i.e., steadfast followers of her Son. We will find Church unity by unity with Him; and to the degree we are united with Him, we will be united also among ourselves. Therefore, let us choose Mary as example, as model and type of our life and of Church life, then we will make steps forward on our ecumenical pilgrimage.

Second, Mary is mother of the Church and of Church unity, because she is our restless intercessor to her Son. To her we can trust our prayers. I know that this is a difficult point for our Protestant and also for many Anglican brothers and sisters. They have problems with the intercession of the saints and also with the intercession of the queen of all saints. They fear that by our prayers to Mary and the saints the unique role and place of Christ as the only and very head of the Church and the only source of all grace could be put into question.

The Second Vatican Council highlighted that our veneration for Our Lady and our trust in her does not diminish or undermine but wants to underline Christ as unique head and the only source of grace. And Mary does not want to be anything apart from or without Christ; she is his first disciple and God's humble handmaid. But as any mother would intercede for her children, and any mother after her death would not cease to intercede in heaven and from heaven, so also Mary accompanies the Church in its pilgrimage and its journey on an often stormy sea with her motherly care. And I am convinced she accompanies the Church also on her way and pilgrimage toward full communion. In her, our mother we can trust.

She stands with us under the cross and feels with us all the suffering of our divisions; she guides us from Good Friday to Easter and to Easter new life and light. She is the mother of hope.

V.

We started by saying that Mary is for us a witness of grace and hope. So let me say as a conclusion some words on hope. Mary is the woman of blessed hope. In good hope she carried the child in her womb through the mountains to her cousin Elizabeth; under the cross she did not despair; she did not run away as the male disciples except John did; steadfast she stood under the cross, because she believed that nothing is impossible for God. So she with the other women was among the apostles and disciples after the ascension of the Lord praying for the coming of the promised Spirit. She remained till the end the woman of hope for the final coming of the kingdom of God. She knew: not the powers of evil, of injustice, hatred and falsehood, God only will speak the last word and then justice will prevail over injustice, love prevail over hatred and truth prevail over all falsehood.

Such hope, founded not in superficial optimism but in God's fidelity, is what we need on our ecumenical pilgrimage. We cannot run away and give up when difficulties arise and immediate success is not at hand. In ecumenism as well as in all Church life we have to pass often the tunnel of darkness in order to come to Easter light. So we need Mary's hope. Hope we need also in our world today. Hope today has become in short supply. There is a lack of perspective and we walk often in the fog and in the mist. But without hope, nobody, no people and the Church neither can live; without hope there is no enthusiasm, no courage for the great goals and great aspirations.

Let us therefore look to Our Lady, the woman of blessed hope, let us learn from her, let us pray to her, let us follow her, because she points and guides to Jesus her son as the light of the world, the way, the truth and the life. She is the dawn and the morning star, announcing the rising sun. She is accompanying us, helping us, guiding us, encouraging us to what Jesus prayed for and left us as his testament: that all be one.

© Walter Kasper, 2008

Paper presented by the Most Reverend Rowan Williams
Archbishop of Canterbury

IN HIS TWO WORKS about the beginning of the Christian Church, St Luke starts by focusing our attention not only on the figure of Mary but on the Holy Spirit. When the angel comes to make his annunciation to Mary, he promises that the Holy Spirit will overshadow her; and when at the beginning of the Acts of the Apostles the disciples gather in the upper room to await the promise of the Father, the Holy Spirit, Mary is in the midst of them. St Luke seems to wish to underline for us that somehow there is a connection between understanding the role of Mary and understanding the Holy Spirit.

Why might this be? St Paul tells us that the Holy Spirit is the creator of *koinonia*, the creator of communion. The Holy Spirit creates in us relationship with Jesus Christ and thus creates in us relationship with one another. As we are bound together in the Spirit we are bound to Jesus Christ: as we are bound to Jesus Christ, we discover our eternal union with God the Father, through the prayer of Christ shared with us in the Holy Spirit. And that may give us a clue to understanding the significance of Mary in St Luke's two texts. The Spirit overshadows Mary, creating in her body a relationship with Jesus. The first human relationship with Jesus Christ is a material one; it is the child growing in Mary's womb. As soon as that relationship with Jesus Christ, the Word Incarnate, is there in the flesh of Mary, Mary goes to share that relationship as she travels to visit Elizabeth. Mary, in receiving relationship with Jesus Christ, receives the possibility of creating relationship with others in Christ to the Father through the power of the Spirit. Mary extends that reality of relationship to those around her. I believe that that is why at the beginning of the Acts of the Apostles, we are given that apparently casual reference to the Mother of Jesus, just to remind us that as the disciples wait for the Spirit, for the promise of the Father, Mary is among them. Her relationship with Jesus continues to be a relationship with the disciples as they wait for the gift of the Spirit; she who has known the fullness of the Spirit's gift, waits with them and, we might say, in her prayer and her attention, prepares the way in the whole fellowship of the disciples for receiving the Spirit at Pentecost. And if we turn to the gospel of St John the same principle is evidently at work. As Mary stands under the cross, it is her relationship with Jesus, that by Jesus' own gift is shared with the 'beloved disciple', who stands for the Church.

So if we are to think about Mary in relationship to the unity of the Church, I believe we need to think about Mary in relation to the Holy Spirit. We need to see this in the gift of the Spirit to Mary – both at the Annunciation and as she prays among the apostles at Pentecost – as the one in whom relationship with Jesus takes its root and begins to spread. It's significant, I believe, that after the story of the Annunciation we do not in any of the Gospels simply meet Mary alone: we meet her with Jesus' family, we meet her among the women and with the beloved disciple at the cross, we meet her in the midst of the apostolic band. But it's as if we never meet her without communion, without her living in communion with all those others called by the Spirit, transformed by the Spirit into friendship with Jesus Christ. So that is my first point. Unity is of course never an abstract reality, it is the community of persons; and therefore to think about unity in connection with Mary is to think about Mary's very specific, very material relationship with Jesus, which then is shared with others.

And so let's focus just for a moment on this significance that is to be found in the relationship with Jesus not being abstract. When God's people relate to Jesus Christ, they do not relate to an idea or an ideal, they don't even relate to a distant memory: they relate to a bodily person in material history; and unless there is that relationship with the material, historical actuality of Jesus, our faith is thin and empty, it becomes a faith which is essentially just about our ideas (and the one thing the Gospel is not is a reaffirmation of the brightest and the best ideas that human beings have had!). And in this respect once again we are reminded, perhaps rather uncomfortably, that the unity of Christians is much more than a unity of ideas. It's no accident that the greatest New Testament image for the unity of Christians is the Body of Christ: because that first relationship with Jesus that we encounter in the New Testament is the deeply material relationship of Mary to the child she carries.

And whatever is true of our unity and our relation with Christ and with one another in the Church, it is somehow more like that kind of unity, that kind of blood within an organism, than it is like the agreement of individuals about their ideas. Our Lady becomes both the supreme example and the supreme symbol of life shared with Jesus Christ, a life shared not in the mind but in flesh and blood, not by hearing words alone, but by that sacramental life of the Church which binds us together as we eat the same food and are held together in that organic reality which is Christ's body.

So as Mary tells us something about communion and its centrality in the communication of Christ's life, and as Mary shows us a pattern of the outpouring of the Spirit immediately creating relationship with Christ in those around, so too Mary reminds us that that relationship is deeper than ideas alone. Mary points us towards that sacramental life in which we truly become Christ's body, over and over again becoming what we already are, becoming what (as St Augustine says) is 'on the table and in the cup', that single reality is both what we are and where we are.

And so, from our contemplation of how Mary is portrayed to us in the New Testament, we can deduce a number of significant points for our understanding of our faith – our faith in common – and what we can hope for in the future in the faith of a Church drawn together in true unity. We can rightly be reminded; first of all, that faith is never an individual matter. When the Spirit kindles the life of Christ in us it is at once a life that is shared and always to be shared: never a possession to be clung to, a talent to be buried in the ground, always a gift to be given. Which of course reminds us of something human beings in their ordinary pride and self-satisfaction don't very much like: we don't really enjoy being dependent. Indeed, in our culture, the greatest value that some people believe in is independence, a total autonomy, not being in debt to another for anything. And yet, of course, we are always as human beings in debt: in debt for our very lives to our parents; in debt for all we understand of humanity or divinity to those around us; in the debt of love to all those who matter to us; and in our life of faith, in debt to the Incarnate Word, born of Mary. Mary does not let us get away with fantasies of independence. As St Paul well knew (and it's an image he uses more than once) our faith needs 'mothering', and to be born afresh of the Spirit, requires that human love, consent and solidarity which brings us as believers to maturity.

What unites us as Christians, is the Holy Spirit of Jesus Christ. Our unity is not a matter of the plans we formulate, the forms of words we can manage to agree about. We need that work – and heaven knows we need it in our day as much as ever, if not more – and yet the unity that matters, the unity that Mary has with Jesus and with Jesus' friends, depends on the Spirit and is deeper than any human achievement. As we pray and search for unity, we have to do it in the openness of prayer, not in the anxiety of planning alone. If our unity rests in the Spirit and is renewed by the Spirit, there is a certain insecurity (which again we know very well) which means we have not to rely on what we can do, but on what God alone can achieve in the Spirit.

Our unity in and through the Spirit is a unity with the Jesus of actual material history, a Jesus truly born of the Virgin, truly vulnerable and human, truly walking in flesh and blood the roads of Galilee, truly and terribly suffering, truly risen from the dead in glorified bodily form. Our union with Jesus is neither the memory of a distant figure in the past now unfortunately dead, or a unity with some idealized humanity which mysteriously mirrors only our own best ideals. It is a union with the strange, transcendent, sometimes frightening, eternal life of this human being in whom the life of the Second Person of the Trinity was completely alive. So, we are united, Mary reminds us, in relation to that reality and no other. And when any Christian family loses sight of that deeply specific anchored reality of the Incarnate Christ, then I'm not at all sure we can have any vital theological view of our unity at all. And we will end up with an idea of the Church that is a great deal less than it should be. United in dependence; united in the Spirit not by our own effort; united in relation to Jesus as material, historical and actual: and if all that seems to imply a certain doctrine of the Resurrection then the seeming is quite accurate. I don't think we can have any doctrine of the Church unless we believe in the Resurrection as portrayed for us in the New Testament: an empty tomb, and no dead body but a living person.

To hold us to this and remind us of this constantly, we have to think of our unity as bound up with the sacramental and visible society that mediates and tells this history over and over again, and that brings us into relationship day by day with the actuality of Jesus, incarnate and risen. Our unity is about a sacramental, visible, historical and material set of relationships. And that means that our quest and our prayer for unity has always to be a quest and a prayer for *visible* unity. There are times – and perhaps our own times are among them – when it's almost tempting to say, 'If only we were not bound to a quest for visible unity.' It would be so much simpler if we could just say that we all have the same ideals and the same general aspirations, but we don't really have to get to the point where we have to share the same table and the same actual fellowship. How much easier, and sadly, how much less than the New Testament sets before us!

If we take seriously the role of Mary in our thinking about unity, we are bound, I believe, to consider how her model of relation with Christ in the Spirit, drives us back to that conviction that we have to seek, however hard, however long the way, for a unity that is indeed organic and real and visible. We may again at times have very little clear sense of what that might be, let alone how to get there, yet that is our prayer.

And so, in conclusion, I would sum up by saying that thinking about Mary in relation to the unity of the Church is one essential way of breaking down false spiritualization and pseudo-spirituality – a reminder that the Holy Spirit is mysteriously much more interested than we often are in bodies and history, in Mary and the disciples, in the suffering and risen flesh of Christ, in the sacraments. That is how and where we encounter the Holy Spirit – not in the privacy of our own skulls, let alone our own feelings. Breaking down that false spiritualization takes us back to seeing how the unity of Christ's people springs to life in the human actuality of the Visitation (the gospel at the Eucharist earlier today) and Pentecost, Luke's two great images. Mary, overshadowed by the Spirit, rushes to communicate with her cousin; Mary in the midst of the disciples waits for the promise of the Father that will break down the boundaries of understanding and racial and ethnic and linguistic difference; Mary waiting for and acting out the new world, the new humanity that the Spirit brings to being, the incarnation and death and resurrection of our Lord Jesus Christ.

© Rowan Williams
September, 2008

> A brief period of questions began with the Bishop of Tarbes and Lourdes inviting both speakers to comment on the prophecy spoken by Simeon of Mary, *'A sword shall pierce through your own soul also'* (Luke 2:35) and its connection with the unity of the Church.

Cardinal Kasper:
First of all I want to thank His Grace for his words: I have nothing to add. These are additional points to what I had to say and I think we totally agree and I also wanted to underline the relationship between Mary and the Spirit, which is very important. The Spirit is the Spirit of Jesus Christ and a concrete sacramental reality: therefore we are aiming for complete visible and sacramental unity of the Church. As the words of old Simeon tell us, Mary's heart is pierced by the sword and she suffers also. She suffered with her son, she is suffering with the mystical body of her son which is the Church. Therefore we must not be content with the reality of divisions within the Church: this must be a reality of suffering for us all. Everybody must do all they can in prayer and suffering, towards the full, visible unity of the Church. I am so happy to see this pilgrimage of Catholics and Anglicans, and we cannot regard division in the Church as normal, ordinary or 'business as usual'.

Archbishop Williams:
I think the words of Simeon to Mary about the sword are indeed a kind of prophecy that if the Incarnate Son of God is indeed an incarnate body, that body can be wounded. And if that is true of our Lord in his earthly life and his passion, it's true in a sense, of his mystical body, also. And I know there have been theologians in the past who have written and reflected about the wounds of the Church

(Rosmini in particular, The Five Wounds of the Church, for example), but without wanting to go into the historical detail of that set of ideas and debates, I think we have to be aware that on the one hand the Church is always capable of being wounded by the infidelity and the betrayal of its own members, by division, by the heightening of hostility and suspicion and violence between believers: and yet always capable of being wounded, always capable of being healed because it is what it is because it is the Body of Christ. And once again our hope has to rest at that level, and we don't simply shrug our shoulders and say 'The Body of Christ is vulnerable: what did you expect?' This is a body that has within it a constantly self-renewing life, moving us more deeply than we can often tell.

The Revd Prebendary David Houlding SSC, one of the Anglican pilgrims, asked:

Your Eminence, Your Grace: you have spoken about the miracle of ecumenism and those of us who were present this morning certainly felt that something very extraordinary was happening. To see you and our Archbishop together in that way was very moving, as well as having one of our newest Church of England deacons vested and reading the Gospel. We're deeply grateful to you for that and I'm sure I speak on behalf of everyone here today.

As you know, Your Eminence, we are a group of Catholic Anglicans who hold the great tradition of the first millennium of the Church most dearly. And it's to that tradition that we seek to witness within our Church of England.

But as you are both aware, we are at this present moment in deep travail, and I know that Archbishop Rowan is particularly sensitive to where we are at the moment, he understands the nature of our predicament. But you've also given us a vision of a common table between Roman Catholics and Anglicans, of communion, that must be at the centre of our ecumenical vision. And I wonder if you could both address a word of hope to us in our present difficulties and suggest how we might renew that vision for a common table and shared communion between us.

Cardinal Kasper:
Well I think what we all experienced today is already a sign of hope, because I could not imagine such an event twenty or thirty years ago. Praying together is very important: the fact that the Archbishop of Canterbury and myself could celebrate – even if not in a full sense – together this morning, is a sign of hope. The ecumenical movement is a pilgrimage and we have to go on in prayer and trust in the Spirit, and also Our Lady will help us. The ecumenical movement is not a means of empire-building, but a movement in the Holy Spirit united with Jesus Christ in his commandments, his life: and sharing his cross and resurrection which will unite us. We need to learn again what Mary told us and go back to the gospels and to the Fathers, which we have in common. We Catholics have a thousand years in common with the Orthodox, but fifteen-hundred years with you, and we should renew our common heritage of the Fathers.

Back at the Lambeth Conference, I spoke of a new Oxford Movement as not only a liturgical movement but a theological movement, to go back to the Fathers. That's our common ground. And from this common ground we can come together at the first millennium which links us also with the Orthodox brothers and sisters. Also at the Lambeth Conference, I was impressed by the attitude of listening to each other. These *indaba* groups listening to each other, I found very moving, and in listening to each other they listened to the Spirit and the good news of the Gospel. The Spirit of Christ guides the Church in the development of dogmas, and we have to regain all this richness and not run off into narrow positions. We must open our hearts for Christ and for the whole of our common tradition, and if we do this, and we do it in a humble way as Mary did, I would trust in the future of the ecumenical movement.

Archbishop Williams:
I think that we mustn't lose sight of the fact that between the Anglican Communion and the Roman Catholic Church there remains, as the Cardinal has said, a real and substantial body of agreed method and vision in theology. It's what is represented by the ARCIC documents right from the beginning to the most recent (though I think some would have questioned aspects of the method

of some of the more recent ones, but that's another story). There remains that heritage which we have acknowledged in common and I've said more than once – so forgive me for saying it again – that it's very important that, in our current debates, developments and experiments towards change, we should constantly be asking the question 'Are we still using the same method of theology? Do we still hold ourselves accountable to the same standards of revealed truth or are we saying theological discussion is a luxury?'

I think we are rather in danger at times of losing sight of that, and failing to ask whether we are still using the same methods. Because once we've stopped speaking the same language in some way, we can't have the debates. Now I think it's important that the Roman Catholic Church and other churches including ours, go on having a real and vigorous debate about the nature of the Petrine office: but in order to have that debate we need to be able to recognize in each other the same language, idiom and rhythm of argument. If that's not there, we can't even begin to have that encounter. And so that means we more and more isolate ourselves from each other.

So, if I'm speaking of hope, I would tell you not to underrate the amount we do have from the last few decades in terms of agreed method and vision, even on the contested subject of ministry: but also on authority and tradition, on many ethical issues, and on Mary; don't underrate that. It needs defending and fighting for within our Anglican context at the moment, but there it is and it hasn't been overturned. I would also say in terms of hopefulness, that the ways of God are deeply mysterious in the economy of the Church: that just as one bit of the Church seems to be losing its nerve about something, some other bit of the Church is discovering it.

It is premature to believe that God has given up on the Anglican Communion, and so if what I've said about the gift of God and the commitment of God is true there will be something that has been given to us as Anglicans historically that we can with humility share with the wider Catholic Christian fellowship. But for that to happen we do need to draw back from those hasty, exclusive often reactive policies and moments where we seem to be veering towards losing the common language. It's a cliché but I think it's true, 'You can only have a useful disagreement when you're speaking the same language' and our danger in Anglicanism is very often that we're losing even the language in which to disagree and that is tragic because it's not only Anglicans who suffer, it's the entire fellowship of all those with whom we would want to have an engaged and robust conversation about all manner of things.

But finally, our hope lies in God's commitment to the Church. Who knows how that will work out in our Anglican context? But it's there, always, and it's expressed in that deposit of common thinking and praying and vision that is still established within our Anglican spectrum. God grant it stays there.

Sermon by the Rt Revd Andrew Burnham
Bishop of Ebbsfleet

Isaiah 66:10-14, John 2:1-11

ON MY BOOKSHELVES I have evidence of an early interest in Lourdes: *The Voice of Lourdes, A Pilgrimage in vision and recorded Sound* was published in 1962. I was fourteen at the time and, a nervous traveller, wondered if I should ever make it.

We pilgrims have travelled here to discover what we already know. That Our Lady of Lourdes is none other than Our Lady of Walsingham. She is also Our Lady of Fatima, Our Lady of Rocamadour and a host of other places, including some 70 or 80 famous icons of Our Lady in the Orthodox world, all associated with particular places and many thought to have miraculous powers. If I go to Sainsbury's, or a Leclerc Hypermarché, I tend to go to the nearest one. Why would I travel several hundred miles? Why bother with Lourdes if we've got Walsingham? Aren't we in danger of a pagan attitude to place? Aren't we in danger of seeing another Mary here, a different one from the one we've got at home? Is there anything on special offer here, something to justify all this travelling?

Jesus, of course, is Lord of this and every place. He is the Creator of all things – the *Pantocrator* – universally revered. But, in the

Gospels, we do have four different accounts of the life of Jesus. They are similar enough for us to realise that they are the life of the same person. They are different enough for us to realise that there is such a thing as 'Matthew's Jesus', 'the Jesus of John'. There is even something of the same in S. Bernadette's accounts: most of what seems to have been said during the fortnight of appearances that began with the fourth appearance, according to one of Bernadette's versions, seems to have been said at the third appearance. These discrepancies are part of the authenticity: in real life there is untidiness of this kind, as anyone who can't find their car keys and then finds them somewhere unexpected knows.

One of the values of the different shrines of Mary is that they highlight not only different cultures and customs but different mysteries. The Lady introduced herself to Bernadette as the Immaculate Conception. Our Lady of Fatima was revealed by a miracle of the dancing sun, Our Lady gloriously assumed. Our Lady of Walsingham whom we shall solemnly celebrate this week, reminds us particularly that Our Lady is the Mother of the Child whom she carries in her arms, a potent reminder of the Incarnation.

And, of course, we always remember that Mary points to Jesus. The first thing the Lady did when Bernadette first saw her was make the sign of the cross. Later, it was on the feast of the Annunciation – when we recall how Mary conceived the Child Jesus in her womb – that Mary revealed herself to Bernadette to be the Immaculate Conception. She was immaculately conceived by God's grace only so that she could conceive and bear him who, in his very Being, is God's grace.

We are welcomed today by Mother Church, by Jerusalem our Mother, by Mary our Mother, 'to suck and be satisfied with her consoling breasts', as Isaiah says. We pilgrims are invited to 'drink deeply with delight from the abundance of her glory'. I want to suggest, from today's Gospel, one over-arching title for Our Lady. She may be Our Lady of Lourdes today and Our Lady of Walsingham on Wednesday, but she is always Our Lady of Cana, Our Lady of the Wedding Feast. Here, as always at Mass, we have a foretaste of the Supper of the Lamb; prefigured in the Wedding Feast of today's Gospel, 'the first miracle that Christ wrought, in

Cana of Galilee'. It is at the eucharistic feast that we feed at the breast and drink with delight.

As English pilgrims, we do well to greet Lourdes with some words of the Venerable Bede. Speaking of the Wedding Feast at Cana he says: 'By this sign [Christ] made manifest that he was the King of glory, and so the church's bridegroom. He came to the marriage as a common human being, but as Lord of heaven and earth he could convert the elements as he wished. How beautifully appropriate it is that when he began the signs that he would show to mortals while he was still mortal he turned water into wine. [But] when he had become immortal through his resurrection, he began the signs that he would show only to those who were pursuing the goal of immortal life.... Therefore let us love with our whole mind, dearly beloved, the marriage of Christ and the church, which was prefigured in one city and is now celebrated over the whole earth'.[1]

And as we celebrate this Marriage Feast let us rejoice that the Mother of Jesus is here to intercede with her Son, as she did at Cana, and to say to us his servants, 'Do whatever he tells you'. If we do, he will surely manifest his glory in our midst and we, his disciples, shall believe in him.

[1] *Homilies on the Gospels* 1:14 ed. Elowsky, Ancient Christian Commentary on Scripture NT IVA John 1-10, IVP Illinois 2006

Sermon by the Rt Revd Geoffrey Rowell
Bishop of Gibraltar in Europe

'The glory which you gave to me I have given them; that they may be one, even as we are one.' (John 17.22)

POPE JOHN PAUL II said on a number of occasions that the church had two lungs, East and West, and it needed to breathe with both of them. I want therefore to begin with the East.

At the end of the thirteenth century a wonderful series of frescoes was painted in the Church of the Mother of God Peribleptos in the city of Ohrid, tucked away in the south-west corner of Macedonia near the Albanian border. Ohrid was in those days a great centre of Christian learning and is still a treasury of Christian art. In the narthex there is a large fresco of Moses first approaching and then taking off his shoes at the burning bush and then, in the top right hand corner, reaching out on the mountain to receive the tablets of the law. In the centre of the burning bush is the angel of the Lord addressing Moses, and at its very heart the Virgin and the child with hand outstretched in blessing. The bush was ablaze with the glory of God's presence, and yet the bush was not burnt.

The artist would have known the ancient Christian tradition sung in the chants of the Orthodox church – 'Moses recognised in the bush the great Sacrament of your birth.' 'What in the Old Testament was a burning bush, in the New Testament was announced through the secret of the Virgin.' (St Gregory of Nyssa) When Mary is called to be the Mother of the Incarnate Son, the angel speaks of how the Holy Spirit will come upon you, and the power of the Most High shall overshadow you. When the Word becomes flesh the glory of God, tabernacles among us. The hymns of the Christian centuries marvel in awe that the God who dwells in light inapproachable, whose glory none can see and live, is a glory of self-giving love that comes down into our human condition, down into the Virgin's womb; down to the very lowest part of our need. The bush was burnt and was not consumed. Mary carried within her the word incarnate, and becomes the 'gate of heaven's high Lord, the door through which the light has poured.' By her humble obedience, and by God's grace, she shares in and is not consumed by the burning fire of divine love within her. John Henry Newman puts it like this:

> "In Jesus Christ is the fullness of the Godhead with all its infinite sanctity. In Mary is reflected the sanctity of Jesus, as by His grace it could be found in a creature... Her very image is a book in which we may read at a glance the mystery of the Incarnation, and the mercy of the Redemption; and withal her one gracious perfections also, who was made by her Divine Son the very type of humility, gentleness, fortitude, purity, patience, love".

The divine glory dwelling in Mary, the glory of that love shown in its fullness in the arms nailed to the cross embracing you and me and the whole human race, the glory that exalts her, as it no less exalts us. The glory which belongs to Jesus, the Word Incarnate, is the glory of the Holy and Blessed Trinity, the glory which is the outpouring in love of the Father's very being, and the life-giving Spirit who is the love and very love-knot of the Trinity. There is no other glory than this. Is the presence of this glory that creates in Mary the love which cares for Christ her Son; which enables our brothers and sisters in the East to speak of the protecting veil of the Mother of God, and of her intercession. It is this glory which our Lord gave to his apostles, gave to us, gave to the church, that wonderful and sacred mystery. This was Mary's life, this is your life, this is our life – this life of transforming grace which changes us from glory into glory. 'God became man, so that man might become God' – so sharply and starkly S. Athanasius put it.' We are to become by grace what He [Christ] is by nature,' as S. Maximus said. And if that is our destiny then it is a single destiny. Unity, communion, our koinonia, is no less than that which binds us into the circling love of God. We come to this place to be touched again by this, As T. S. Eliot puts it in 'East Coker' in his *Four Quartets:*

We must be still and still moving,

Into another intensity

For a further union, a deeper communion.

We are about communion, not federation; about the life of God, not organisation. Mary, who, as Hopkins says, 'has but one work to do, to let God's glory through', is and can only be a channel of that unity, because she is the channel of God's glory. As we come as a church, divided in pilgrimage, to this holy place, we come to ask her prayers, to ask that she spreads over us her protecting veil, that we may be gathered into the unity which is only found and known in the body of the Son which she bore, the Word of God, who through her proceeding forth, yet leaveth not his Father's side. Mark Frank, preaching in the 17th century on Christmas Day, said simply 'By this day's emptiness we all were filled.' It is through self-emptying that we are filled; the self-emptying of God, coming down to the lowest part of our need; the self-emptying of Blessed Mary in humble obedience; our self-emptying as we stretch out our hands, our needs, our sorrow and our joy, to be transformed by that glory which will transfigure, transform, and bind us together in the unity which is God's will for his church, and which reveals his glory to the world.

Sermon by the Revd Philip North
Priest Administrator
The Shrine of Our Lady of Walsingham

Now before the festival of the Passover, Jesus knew that his hour had come to depart from this world and go to the Father. Having loved his own who were in the world, he loved them to the end. The devil had already put it into the heart of Judas son of Simon Iscariot to betray him. And during supper Jesus, knowing that the Father had given all things into his hands, and that he had come from God and was going to God, got up from the table, took off his outer robe, and tied a towel around himself. Then he poured water into a basin and began to wash the disciples' feet and to wipe them with the towel that was tied around him. He came to Simon Peter, who said to him, 'Lord, are you going to wash my feet?' Jesus answered, 'You do not know now what I am doing, but later you will understand.' Peter said to him, 'You will never wash my feet.' Jesus answered, 'Unless I wash you, you have no share with me.' Simon Peter said to him, 'Lord, not my feet only but also my hands and my head!' Jesus said to him, 'One who has bathed does not need to wash, except for the feet, but is entirely clean. (John 13. 1-10)

I WENT TO A SCHOOL in North London that was equally divided between Spurs fans and Arsenal fans. We lived together in an uneasy truce. The Spurs fans longed to beat up the Arsenal fans, but they knew that if they did, they'd have half the school beating them up. And it also worked vice versa. It was a kind of cold-war style stand off which no one had the nerve to breach. I have vivid memories, however, of a new first year turning up. He was weedy, pathetic boy, a bit like Fr Philip Barnes, and he was asked in the boys' lavs whether he was Spurs or Arsenal, and he replied, 'Oh I don't much care for football.' It was fabulous. At last we had found someone we could all beat up without any fear of reprisal. That silly boy had made the foolish error of living on the boundary.

We love clear boundaries. We love strong, firm distinctions to be drawn between groups of people or nations or ethnic groups. And we feel deeply threatened when those boundaries are breached. One clear boundary that we draw up is that between those who are sick and those who healthy. You generally have to be one or the other. The sick are weak. The healthy are strong. The sick are those who are cared for. The healthy do the caring. The sick are the recipients. The healthy are the givers. The sick lie in bed. The healthy turn up with the grapes, eat them and then get bored. You are either sick or healthy. You may move from one category to the other, but you may not be both. Until, that is, you come to Lourdes.

Tina Beattie wrote a fascinating article in 'The Tablet' last week in which she spoke of Lourdes as a place of 'liminality.' Anyone who has moved house, changed job, been on a long journey or met new friends has had an experience of liminality. The liminal place is the threshold, the place of new experience, the place where boundaries are breached, the place which is both and neither. And because of that, the points of liminality in our lives are the points of greatest challenge, of change, of growth, of personal development. We fear the liminal, but at the same time we need it in order to become most fully ourselves.

Lourdes is profoundly a place where boundaries are breached. Just think of the experiences of the past few days where boundaries between and within our churches have been breached again and again. But it seems to me that the boundary that is most vividly breached at Lourdes is that between the sick and the healthy. In this place the sick, who are so often marginalised, sidelined, silenced and dumped in faceless institutions, come first. They go at the front of processions, they get the best treatment, the best of everything. The weak are the strong. Here we live to Kingdom values and so those who are powerful in the eyes of the world are left to wait at the back of the queue.

But this role reversal goes further. Here, in the place of liminality, the sick minister to the healthy, showing us that sickness is not just something to be cured of, but is part of the mystery of life. Here the sick are the givers and the healthy are the recipients. Here the sick show the healthy how to live the Christian life. To see how, just reflect for a moment on the Gospel we heard earlier. This scene of Jesus washing the disciples feet in one of intense liminality in every sense. Every boundary is being breached here as Jesus prepares the disciples for his death. And now, the one who is Lord and Master takes the role of a slave. The eternal word washes the feet of his motley crew of disciples. What is fascinating is Peter's reaction. He can't bear the thought. 'You won't wash my feet!' Peter is the loyal disciple. The thought of Jesus acting towards him as if he were a slave is intolerable. But Jesus' answer is shocking in its forcefulness. 'Unless I wash you, you have no share with me.' To minister in his name, Peter must first let Jesus minister to him. Unless he opens his heart to receive, he cannot give.

And that is the great truth that, in Lourdes, the sick demonstrate to the healthy. Most of us love to care for those around us. We love to minister to others. We love to serve. On one level, that's fabulous. And let's face it, by doing so we win affection, and we put ourselves in control, in the position of power. But how easy do we find it to receive? So often I find myself talking to elderly people who, in their frailty, need to be cared for after a lifetime spent doing the caring. And they can't manage it. They can't bear what they see as the affront to their pride. But Christian ministry begins when we allow ourselves to be not the ministers but the recipients of care. Only when we allow Christ to wash our feet can we wash the feet of the world. Only when we allow ourselves to be ministered to can we be liberated to minister to others. Remember the old wives tale 'It is better to give than to receive?' It's rubbish. It's only once we have received from Christ that we can give to the world.

As we gather for this liturgy, here there are no boundaries, no distinction between healthy and sick. This is the place of liminality. Here we are all alive with good health. Here we are all profoundly diseased. And here we open ourselves up to receive the touch of Christ. Here Our Lord and Master, the eternal word of the father, stoops to touch us and minister to us. Here he serves us as he served the disciples before the Last Supper. So let us open our hearts to receive the ministry of Christ. For only when we have received can we go back home to minister to the world.

Sermon by the Rt Revd Robert Ladds
Superior-General
The Society of Mary

THIS SPECIAL and holy place of Bétharram is a Shrine of Our Blessed Lady far more ancient than Lourdes. It was known and frequented by S. Bernadette. Like many an ancient Church and holy place it has been through many ups and downs and been subject to destruction. The name "Bétharram" is derived from the local Bearn dialect, the words "bet arram" meaning "beautiful branch" and that name tells directly of the origins of the Shrine. The miracle of the Beautiful Branch relates to that turbulent river you will have seen flowing past this Church; a young girl fell into the flood and was swept away and, in spite of efforts to save her, was thought to be lost. She was later found safe on the river bank and told of a Vision of Our Lady, leaning over the waters and holding out the branch of a tree for her to cling to and come to safety.

Certainly Christians have clung to Bétharram and its message over these many years. Before the beginning of the 16th century this place was much visited and during the 17th century the Shrine of Our Lady of the Beautiful Branch was a great place of pilgrimage and devotion.

The Huguenots burnt the ancient chapel in 1569 and the re-built Church was not spared by the French Revolution. S. Michael Garicoïts (whose Relics and Shrine you will see in the retro-chapel) brought the Shrine back to life in the first half of the 19th century and founded here the Order of Priests of the Sacred Heart; which Priests continue to minister throughout the world to-day. He persuaded Napoleon III and the Empress Eugène to restore the Church and some of that renewing we see in this remarkable place to day.

The message here is, surely, two-fold. The original message of the miracle of the Beautiful Branch offered by Our Lady that is life-saving. The second message is one of continuity. This holy place, through good times and bad, in spite of destruction, continues to reveal the same and the constant message of the life-line offered by God to all who will but reach out and hold fast.

"Then a branch will grow from the stock of Jesse, and a shoot will extend from his roots". Perhaps we are in danger of hearing those wonderful words, full of promise, written by Isaiah, (Is 11:1) too often at carol services to appreciate their utter wonder.

"In the fullness of time" – that is, in God's good time and for all time and beyond time – the righteous branch, Christ Jesus, was, as it were, held out to us by God through Our Lady Mary. And, just as Isaiah foretold, it was indeed a truly beautiful branch: "in that day the branch of the Lord shall be a beautiful branch; it will become glorious in its beauty and the fruit of the land shall be the pride and splendour of the survivors of the Lord's people." (Is 4:2)

The Lord Himself teaches us that no branch can survive and bear fruit except it remain constant and a part of Him in life and in faith (John 15:4-6). If the branch does not abide in Him it fades and dies. Our Blessed Lady gives us the example of constancy and abiding; She it was who followed Her Son even to the Foot of His Cross. Mary bears fruit. First, the fruit of Her Womb Jesus and, as Her children, we know and experience that fruit in Her care and through Her prayers.

Such constancy in the faith of Christ and to the life of His Holy Catholic Church is the calling of all. It has been the calling of those Christians who have come before us here to Bétharram. In refreshing their faith at the place of the "Beautiful Branch" they have had confidence to remain faithful, to re-make and re-build not only this physical shrine but also the spiritual shrine of their own lives. This is our calling too.

How moving and remarkable it is that the child Bernadette came here to Bétharram just four or five days before receiving the Apparitions at Lourdes. How remarkable that the River Gave of the miracle of the Beautiful Branch is that same river flowing past the Grotto of the Lourdes. How remarkable that Bernadette was sent here by Bishop Laurence for the comfort, support and understanding of S. Michael Garicoïts immediately after the apparitions and before any investigations were started.

But perhaps not remarkable at all. Not remarkable at all when considered within the mercy and grace of God. Here countless Pilgrims have been inspired and enabled to reach out again from the drowning torrents of sin, of sorrow, of persecution and of apostasy. And reaching out in faith, as did that child of the ancient miracle, they have found Our Blessed Lady holding out to them the most Beautiful Branch of salvation, even Her Blessed Child, Christ Jesus Our Lord.

Here Bernadette found inspiration, comfort, fortitude and courage for all she would have to endure. Pray that we and others shall continue to find these graces too.

AMEN

This sermon was given on a visit to Bétharram and was part of the Lourdes Pilgrimage.

Mary
A Focus for Unity
for all Christians?

**A pictorial record of the
pilgrimages to Nettuno
and Lourdes in 2008**

Don Carlo, the Parish Priest of S. Giovanni, giving an address on the steps of the church.

Adoration of the Blessed Sacrament by candlelight.

Several gifts were exchanged between the closely-linked towns of Ipswich and Nettuno. This handmade crib, reflecting a mountain village in Southern Italy, was presented to Fr Stephen Raine the Parish Priest of the Church of S. Mary at the Elms, Ipswich – home of the restored Shrine of Our Lady of Grace.

Bishops Robert Ladds *(left)* and Keith Newton with the Mayors of Nettuno and Ipswich in Nettuno Town Hall. Children from S. Mark's RC Primary School in Ipswich which is 'twinned' with the Scuola S. Giovanni in Nettuno. The Prior of the Confraternity of Our Lady of Grace, Mario Mazzanti *(right)*.

A wonderful firework display was part of the festival made more spectacular when reflected in the waters of Nettuno harbour.

Provision was made for Pilgrimage Masses at the Shrine of S. Maria Goretti in the crypt of the Basilica. However, the Rector offered facilities for the Pentecost Mass in the walled garden in front of a shrine of Our Lady of Lourdes. Words are unable to describe the holy atmosphere of that Mass complete with glorious Italian sun.

Bishop Robert Ladds, the Principal Celebrant at the Mass, is pictured on the previous page.

Entry of members of The Confraternity to the Parish Church of S. Giovanni during the celebrations.

The Bishops, Clergy, Members of the Confraternity and the Prioresses in front of the Altar of S. Giovanni.

The Bishops and Prioresses outside S. Giovanni.

Pupils from S. Mark's Primary School assemble on Sunday evening outside S. Filipina's school in readiness for the informal procession to S. Giovanni's. The statue of Our Lady is then taken in an huge procession to the Basilica.

The Procession *en-route* through the streets of Nettuno. Older girls and boys wear their First Communion clothes, while smaller children dress as angels and pageboys in a myriad of colours. There was even a miniature friar and a priest complete with biretta! In the background, are the wonderful illuminated arches constructed for the event.

The Sunday evening procession from S. Giovanni to the Basilica.

The Statue stops on a number of occasions when Our Lady of Grace turns towards the sea, as fireworks are let off on the ramparts of the old town, a tradition dating back many years

On arrival at the Basilica the Statue is carried backward up the steps to face the people. The Statue is greeted by a fanfare of fireworks and bells.

Meeting in the Vatican Offices of the Pontifical Council for Promoting Christian Unity with Mgr Donald Bolen.

The Bishops and Clergy outside the Basilica.

The interior of the Basilica with Our Lady of Grace returned to her throne above the altar.

The English festival of Our Lady of Grace is held annually at the end of May. This is well supported by the Confraternity of Nettuno.

This picture shows the copy of the statue which is in S. Mary at the Elms Ipswich robed for the festival with a visiting Prioress.

The flag of the Archbishop of Canterbury was flown in the Domaine of Lourdes throughout his visit

The arrival of the torchlight procession on the steps of the Rosary Basilica.

The Archbishop of Canterbury, the Most Revd Rowan Williams and The President of the Pontifical Council for Promoting Christian Unity, Cardinal Walter Kasper giving a joint blessing at the conclusion of the torchlight procession at Lourdes.

The Statue of Our Lady of Walsingham was carried in procession at the beginning of the International Mass in the Basilica of S. Pius X.

Likewise the banners of The Society of Mary, The Society of Our Lady of Walsingham, and The National Shrine at Walsingham were carried in procession at the International Mass.

The Deacon, Simon Morris, proclaiming the Gospel in English.

The Archbishop preaching at the International Mass beside Our Lady of Walsingham.

The Ecumenical Conference, hosted by Bishop Jacques Perrier of Tarbes and Lourdes *(left)*, with Cardinal Kasper, and The Archbishop of Canterbury *(right)*.

The Pilgrimage Reception at the Hôtel Eliseo. Cardinal Walter Kasper *(above)* and The Archbishop of Canterbury *(below)* being greeted outside the Hotel.

The Rt Revd Robert Ladds, Superior-General of The Society of Mary, welcoming the distinguished guests to the Reception.

The Archbishop of Canterbury with Cardinal Walter Kasper *(above)* and Bishop Jacques Perrier of Tarbes and Lourdes *(below)*.

Cardinal Walter Kasper *(centre)* with Fr Graeme Rowlands, Chaplain-General and Director of Pilgrimage of The Society of Mary *(left)* and Simon Murray – Mancunia Tours Lourdes Manager *(right)*.

This Statue of Our Lady of Walsingham
was given to the Shrine of Lourdes
in 1984
by the Anglican Society of Mary
in thanksgiving for graces received

Cette statue de Notre Dame de Walsingham
fut présentée aux Sanctuaires de Lourdes
en 1984
par la Société anglicane de Marie
en reconnaissance de grâces reçues